Life,
Law
and not enough shoes

Ian & Enid

Wonderful to meet you

[signature]

Queen Elizabeth
29 February 2016

Life, Law
and not enough shoes

Life as a criminal lawyer
JUDITH FORDHAM

Dedication
For John

First published in Australia in 2008 by
New Holland Publishers (Australia) Pty Ltd
Sydney • Auckland • London • Cape Town
1/66 Gibbes Street Chatswood NSW 2067 Australia
218 Lake Road Northcote Auckland New Zealand
86 Edgware Road London W2 2EA United Kingdom
Wembley Square First Floor Solan Road Gardens Cape Town 8001
Reprinted 2010, 2012

Copyright © 2008 in text: Judith Fordham
Copyright © 2008 New Holland Publishers (Australia) Pty Ltd
All rights reserved. No part of this publication may be reproduced, stored in a retrieval system or transmitted, in any form or by any means, electronic, mechanical, photocopying, recording or otherwise, without the prior written permission of the publishers and copyright holders.

National Library of Australia Cataloguing-in-Publication Data:
    Fordham, Judith.
    Life, law and not enough shoes : life as a criminal
    lawyer / author, Judith Fordham.
    ISBN 9781741105391 (pbk.)
    Includes index.
    Forensic sciences--Australia.
    Criminal investigation--Australia.
    Criminal justice, Administration of--Australia.
    Women lawyers--Australia--Biography.
    Lawyers--Australia--Biography.
    363.25092

Publisher: Fiona Schultz
Editor: Geraldine Coren
Junior Editor: Sally Hills
Managing Editor: Lliane Clarke
Designer: Natasha Hayles
Production Manager: Linda Bottari
Printer: Toppan Leefung Printing Limited
Front cover illustration: Andrew Burchett, Drawing Book Studios
Back cover photo: Flourish magazine

10 9 8 7 6 5 4 3

Acknowledgments

I would like to name here every person in my life who has inspired me but that is impossible. Some have inspired me as teachers, sharing with me the joy and excitement of knowledge, and encouraging me always to question. Roy Wheeler, Keith Lawler, take a bow! Others have inspired by their bravery, irreverent humour, loyalty and pigheadedness. Maree Whitaker, Karin Margolius, Helen Fowler—you are amazing women. To the lady who let me read any book in the library, a thousand thanks.

To my sisters, Jenny and Carol: each of whom has such resilience. Whatever life throws at them they just bounce back! My children: Linda, Maud, Lewis, Anni. Talented and loving human beings of whom I am extremely proud. John, the 'good' husband: chief cook and wine glass washer, without whose support and love I would be lost.

My students, whose learning thrills me. The several lawyers who count me as a mentor: I am honoured, and I promise that no question is too dumb. And, of course, those who have mentored me and have put up with my extremely dumb questions over many years.

My clients: there is something good in each of them, and something to learn from each of them. Without them this book would not have happened at all.

And Linda Williams, this is all your fault!

Foreword

I was more than a little apprehensive when I met Judith. I was facing serious criminal charges and memories of my last legal aid lawyer (a Sikh with full turban but an empty head) were fresh in my mind. I was escorted by a prison guard to the visits room—not another 'lawyer lawyer pants on foiyer', I hoped. While I was discussing the case (through a telephone handset) with this attractive, slightly nervous but self confident lady, it was hard to tell she was as new to this, as I was. After 30 odd minutes, even through the thick, dirty, graffitied bulletproof glass, I sensed her enthusiasm, her REALNESS and her honesty. I felt she understood and, more importantly, she BELIEVED me. Win or lose I knew she would do her absolute best and no-one can ask more than that. That was 18 years ago and Judith has represented me many times since then, and I have nothing but respect for her strength, honesty and sharp legal mind. The nervousness has gone but the enthusiasm remains, and I have never seen her take a backward step in the theatre of war that is our courts. After all these years and all we have seen I think we can both be forgiven for thinking that often truth and justice comes a distant second to the best performance of the day.

Sean Egan
GJMC

Contents

Introduction

The Accidental Lawyer   10

The Flying Lawyer and Other Stories   34

My Life of Crime   51

More Than a Woman   72

He Fell on the Knife   93

Nutters and Nasties   115

Judging Judy   129

Sex and Drugs and Rock 'n' Roll   152

Prison Greens   173

What Happened?   194

Dead Pigs and Forensics   206

From Rats to Chateaux   226

Introduction

Dinner parties have a lot to answer for. So do plane trips. I seem to have packed a lot of strange experiences into my life, particularly over the last 20 years. This gives me much to talk about at dinner parties, and I am exceedingly good at talking. Virtually every time I recount one of these stories someone says 'you should write a book'. I thought that perhaps I would one day when I had nothing else to do, until I realised that day would never come.

Travelling from New Zealand to Sydney a couple of years ago. I sat next to an attractive blonde lady, about my age. A very good age. We ignored each other for most of the flight. I think we were both a bit tired and grumpy. Towards the end we relaxed over a glass of wine and started chatting. The lady, Linda—beautiful, and unfailingly cheerful—eventually suggested, as others had before, that I should write a book about my experiences.

Unlike the others, she managed to get me to promise to do it and told me that she had the contacts to make it happen. She introduced me to my publishers, New Holland, and before I knew it I was the first author in recorded history, or so it seemed, to land a contract without having to hawk a manuscript to 50 publishers first. Spot the mistake! I had to fit the writing of the book into an unbelievably busy life. It required several all-night stints from me and considerable patience on the part of New Holland, for which I thank them.

I have had to tippy-toe around some facts in the stories I have told in this book—names have been changed to protect the guilty as well as the innocent! Where I have felt there might be some danger of identifying someone who might not want to be identified, I have changed facts, names and sometimes even merged locations, people or stories. I have indulged in a little exaggeration and the occasional liberty with the truth. A number of people will identify themselves, I suspect, but these people are likely to be either flattered or amused or both. So here it is: a light-hearted look at life as a 'lady lawyer'.

The Accidental Lawyer

I used to jam a pillow under my bedroom door to try to stop the rats from getting in and biting my toes. They could reach my toes because I slept on a mattress on the floor. I slept on a mattress because I couldn't afford a bed. I couldn't afford a bed because for the previous few years I had been either pregnant or breastfeeding, so my only income was from odd jobs, and selling what few belongings I had left to help support my children, myself and my husband.

I was the first child of parents whose relationship had been dysfunctional from the beginning. Inevitably, then, we were not a close family. My younger sister and I coped in different ways. As the eldest, I bore the brunt of my father's violent temper. My sister turned blending into the background and being inoffensive into an art form, which my nature would never allow me to do. There was a much younger sister who somehow won our father's approval and as a result had a very different childhood. My mother escaped into alcohol and prescription drugs. My parents managed to prevent my sisters and me from becoming close as children, although we are doing our best to make up for lost time now. I had no idea how a normal family functioned, nor any example of a loving adult relationship.

I developed a finely honed sense of personal worthlessness. No matter how hard I tried, whatever I achieved was never good enough. I escaped into reading and study, and did well at school. For as long as I can remember I experienced another life by reading. I read every book in the children's section of the local library and most of the books in the adult section. I volunteered for things: sang in Eisteddfods and school productions, helped edit the school magazine, earned my Bronze Cross in lifesaving and was awarded a scholarship to go to university. No matter, I still felt I wasn't good enough. I was deeply unhappy and insecure.

Since this is a book about crime, I suppose I should confess that when I was about nine years old I fell in love with a gold (well, gold-coloured) bangle. It was designed to spiral around one's arm in the shape of the snake, complete with green eyes set in the snake's head—even then I liked pretty things. It was in the days when Woolworths had all their small items for sale within easy reach on a slightly angled counter with sections marked out by glass dividers.

I came back several days in a row just to look at this masterpiece. In the end, it was too much temptation for a nine-year-old to bear. I stood there in my school uniform gazing at it after school one day. For about 10 minutes I struggled with a combination of fear of the consequences, and the desperate need to have the gold snake bracelet. I can still see the little green eyes and the markings of scales along the length of the bracelet. I wanted it so badly. I reached out my ink-stained hand, with its bitten fingernails, grabbed the bracelet and slipped it into my blazer pocket. Immediately the sales assistant, who'd been watching me all along, told me to give it back.

I was shocked, guilt-stricken, terrified that my father would be told and worried that I would bring disrepute to the school. I gave it back, weeping. I don't think the assistant told anyone. She could see how upset I was. I never, ever did anything like that again.

I left home as soon as I possibly could and married the wrong person—in retrospect, as a way of escaping. At the time I did not recognise that. My first husband, the father of my eldest daughter, is a fine human being, but we drifted apart. Still achieving, I earned my science degree during the marriage. After we divorced, I married the next man who seemed willing. I desperately wanted love and warmth in my life, but I could not believe that anybody would want to marry me: who could possibly want a 26-year-old woman with a child?

My second husband shared a lot of my father's qualities, including the use of violence as a way of communicating with me. Marrying into a violent relationship was not surprising considering what I had learnt about family life as a child. I had no idea how to be happy or assertive and did not even know there were choices I could make other than simply surviving. I stayed for many reasons, including not wanting to be a failure at marriage again, having nowhere to go and no family support to fall back on, and the idea that somehow all of this must be my fault.

Fast forward (skipping lots of horrible stuff): after five years of marriage, I had had two more children—a girl and a boy—and was pregnant with my fourth. Desperation gave me the strength to leave. I moved away and three months later gave birth to my fourth child, a girl. This was a home birth as were all but the birth of my first child.

The next question was what to do in the immediate future. I would be lying if I said I was deciding what to do with the rest of my life. Even today, I'm lucky to have a five-minute plan, let alone a five-year plan. One of my options was to go on a supporting parent pension. Another was to go back to study. Whatever I chose I would need some form of government support for a time. Considering that I had four children, three of them under the age of five, I didn't think this was too much to ask, but I wanted to accept that support for as short a time as possible.

Law school

Law was the only second degree that government support was available for, so I applied, thinking I would never get in. I was accepted as a mature age student and enrolled, thinking I wouldn't be accepted if I tried to enrol the following year.

I would love to say that I had a burning ambition to be a lawyer and save the world, but there was no noble calling, just a need for money, an opportunity, and a woman who had no idea what she was getting herself into. I didn't know anything about being a lawyer. At school I wanted to be an actuary, but only because a teacher had told me I couldn't.

I had met a pregnant lawyer once in a childbirth class. I was ever so impressed, but it seemed somehow wrong: lawyers did not do the things mere mortals did. It was a bit like your mum or the Queen doing 'it'! I always thought being a lawyer was a very glamorous occupation … at least until I became one. So I became a lawyer quite by accident, not because Daddy was a lawyer, or because it was a safe occupation, or because the hours would be better than a doctor's.

Going to law school with the responsibilities I had in my life was unbelievably difficult. I think I slept through more lectures than I listened to. Because I did law in Canberra, the nation's capital, the course was very heavy in constitutional and administrative law, which I found particularly soporific.

One day, shortly before I retire, I intend to say something in court about the 'general vibe' of the Constitution, in homage to one of my favourite movies, *The Castle*. This classic Australian comedy features a battler who takes on the might of the government which wants to resume his home in order to build a new runway for the local airport. Before a kind-hearted QC stepped in to save the day, the battler was represented by his local suburban lawyer, whose best effort was to tell the judge that he could not point to which part of the Constitution of the Commonwealth of Australia he relied upon in his legal argument: it was just the general 'vibe' of it. That will be the only time I will use the Constitution, I suspect.

I held down many part-time and casual jobs while I was at law school, all of which proved good experience for relating to people from all walks of life when I was dealing with clients and jurors in criminal trials. Some of the jobs included being a member of the night staff at a nursing home, cleaning houses and teaching swimming.

I became quite entrepreneurial in my swimming teaching, offering private lessons to children and adults who had resisted any attempts to learn to swim previously, with a 'your money back' deal if the pupil was not swimming by the end of the first lesson. I had a fairly loose definition of 'swimming', but as a good lawyer-to-be I made sure that the person paying for the lessons and I agreed on the definition. I am proud to say I never had to give anyone their money back—and I still remember the joy of seeing an adult take their first strokes, or the mother of an intellectually disabled boy crying with happiness at seeing him afloat.

Sad to say, I didn't get the same joy out of house cleaning! I wasn't particularly good at it, but at least I could bring a baby in a bassinette along with me. As for working in a nursing home, I found being the only person on duty, with a piercing alarm in my room to be sounded by any resident who needed me at 4.30am, just too frightening. The management wanted to save money, so they chose to take on someone completely unqualified for such work. My duties included handing out medication, showering those residents who were not capable of showering themselves, and dealing with any emergency which arose at any time. With only one pair of hands at times, this was at times extremely difficult (and scary: what if someone had died or had a fall on my shift?). My children were looked after by a friend while I was on duty and I wasn't happy about that either. That job did not last.

Work experience

During my last couple of years at law school I approached a criminal law firm and offered to work for them free of charge in order to get some experience. Being older than the average law student, I was lucky enough to be trusted with some responsibility.

The most memorable experience at that firm was being loaned to a Queen's Counsel to help on a murder case. I had never met a QC before, but had certain preconceived ideas from watching the television show *Rumpole of the Bailey*. This man did not disappoint, possessing distinguished grey hair, an impressive physique, a dapper taste in clothing, right down to the gold watch chain, and vowels so rounded I'm surprised he didn't choke on them. He probably ate gravitas for breakfast. I was ever so impressed.

This experience gave me both my first taste of crime and my first taste of forensics. I was never the same again. My duties included researching contrecoup injury (a type of brain injury) and ordering the QC's lunch.

The case involved a man who was charged with murder. The prosecution was saying that the accused struck the victim a fatal blow on the same side of the head as the brain injury, with the victim then falling to the ground and injuring his scalp on the opposite side, while the defence was saying that both injuries came from the one impact suffered in an accidental fall. The strange thing, if the defence claims were correct, was that the bleeding on the surface of the brain was on the opposite side from the impact. With my science background, I enjoyed the medical research. I discovered that contrecoup injury occurs when a person's head hits something solid, and the brain is injured on the opposite side. It has to do with the brain moving around in the skull cavity.

Ordering the QC's lunch involved skills of an entirely different nature. Lunch was between 1pm and 2.15pm. A steakhouse was about a five-minute walk from the court. I was tasked to leave court at exactly 12.30pm, go to the restaurant, order the T-bone, choose a decent bottle of red wine and ensure that it was opened and ready to pour by the time the great man arrived.

On the first day, I had no idea what red wine to order, but fluked a very good one. Instantly I became very popular with His Majesty. I then sat across from him, nibbled on my steak, drank a glass of wine and watched in shock and awe as he polished off the rest of the bottle. The routine was the same each day of the three-week trial, the only variation being the addition of a glass or two of cognac and a cigar if things were going particularly well on the day. The QC would then return to court and function theatrically and magnificently. I would sit behind him with my head spinning, struggling to stay awake. The most important lesson I learnt was never to drink at lunchtime if you are planning to go back into court.

At the end of the trial I was about to fly to Perth for interviews with several firms I had applied to. Almost as an afterthought, I asked the QC if he would give me a reference. He was a flamboyant man, and I received a flamboyant handwritten reference. I carried it to each interview and handed it over at an appropriate moment. When a potential employer reached the portion which read, 'she's no pussycat', there was a remarkable change in the dynamics of the interview. I was asked about the trial, and about just what the QC had meant by this description. The formality immediately disappeared and I was offered a position by every firm which interviewed me. I guess it really is the case that it's not what you know but who you know.

I chose Perth partly because it was one of the few places that offered what is known as a 'fused' profession in the law. That is, you can be a barrister AND a solicitor.

Why did this matter to me?

I knew I wanted to be a courtroom lawyer or barrister, but could not afford to sit around waiting for work. I had three young children to house, clothe and feed. (The fourth had elected to stay with her father in Canberra.)

A barrister is a court lawyer, an advocate who specialises in going to court. All the lawyers working in Western Australia are barristers as well as solicitors and so can go to court and do trials or appeals, if they care to. My admission certificate (that is, my admission to legal practice) says I am a barrister, solicitor and proctor. I have yet to discover what a proctor does. I think it has something to do with bottoms.

A solicitor is a lawyer who generally does not go to court. In the eastern states of Australia, a lawyer has to choose to be one or the other. There, a new lawyer will, if he or she decides to be a barrister, spend the early part of his or her career waiting for work and taking the crumbs that other barristers pass on, until they become known in their own right to solicitors who will send them work (briefs, that is, jobs). The 'baby barrister' is not allowed to deal with clients directly, so must depend on others to send him or her briefs.

I finished my degree, packed up the household and children and moved to Perth. Perth in the 1980s had a 'frontier land' feeling about it. I thought that I could make up for lost time more quickly there than I could have in the more conservative eastern states. I was right.

My older two children were school age, but the youngest was only four. In the east, she would have been able to go to school, but in Western Australia, the school age was a year older. She was already reading and writing. I would like to say that this was the reason I tried so hard to get her into school, but in truth, a major motivation was that I was going to be working full-time and needed the childcare. Luckily for me, the school's numbers were already at critical mass, and only needed one more enrolment before the school could justify a request to the powers that be for an additional staff member.

I made the headmaster an offer: 'Give her six weeks. If she is not coping I will take her out of school.' I knew I would not need to do this and had no intention of doing so. She was just fine, and continued as the youngest in the class throughout her school career. She became a fine athlete, I suspect partly because she did not admit her age and so was always competing in races with children a year older than she was.

Becoming a medical negligence 'expert'

My first job was at a medium-sized firm, mainly doing medical negligence. I started as an articled clerk. This is the one-year apprenticeship which all lawyers must serve before they become 'real' lawyers and are allowed to call themselves barristers or solicitors. I was a little luckier than some new lawyers as I had my own broom cupboard/office, where I displayed my proudest possession, a hot pink stiletto heeled shoe phone. When it rang, I would speak into the sole *à la* Maxwell Smart. I was told by my boss that this was not an appropriate image, which just added to my enjoyment in using it.

Part of the reason I landed this job was because I told the partner who interviewed me that I had drafted my own will. He asked to have a look at it, making it very clear that he expected to be able to tell me what was wrong with it, but he couldn't find any mistakes. Possibly because of that, I was asked to go to a hospital to 'take instructions' for a will. That is, I was supposed to talk to the client, find out what he wanted to achieve in his will and then come back to the office and get a real lawyer to draft it.

The client was dying of cancer. He had had a colourful past. In an eight-bed ward which smelt of death, he wanted to confess a crime, the nature of which I just didn't want to know, and to tell me where a very large amount of money was buried in his backyard. To my eternal regret, I managed to avoid having him tell me either of these things, and simply got the details for his will.

Although I had no medical training, I had a feeling he was not going to last long and decided to hand write the will on the spot and get him to sign it. I asked a doctor to both witness the signing and to write an accompanying letter to say that the client was competent (that is, in his right mind, so he knew what he was leaving to whom) at the time.

I got into all sorts of trouble when I got back to the office for doing this, as I was at the time only an articled clerk or trainee, not yet able to work as a lawyer. A 'proper' will was hurriedly drawn up, by a properly qualified lawyer, but by lunchtime the next day, before anyone had had a chance to go back up to the hospital, the client had died. Suddenly everybody stopped being grumpy at me for what I'd done.

It was during my time with this firm that I came across a doctor with probably the worst bedside manner in the entire universe. His patient rang me from hospital: 'I want to kill the bastard!'

'Which particular bastard would that be? I know several.'

I eventually pieced together what had happened. This patient was a nurse who had gone into hospital for some exploratory surgery. She had been suffering some pain in the region of one of her ovaries. She had specifically told the doctor that unless there was a life or death reason, he was not to do anything to her ovaries. When she came round from the anaesthetic one of the nurses told her that she had had one ovary removed.

When he came to see her on his hospital rounds, she tackled him about it: 'Doctor, I told you not to touch my ovaries.'

The doctor's delightfully sensitive reply was, 'You said *ovaries*, and I only took one out.'

What a sweetheart, a true gentleman. I took great pleasure in taking legal action against him. My client did not need to go to court. The insurance company was very happy to settle the claim out of court. There was a decent sum for the loss of the ovary and a larger sum, called 'hush money' in the trade. That is, the price of avoiding the embarrassment of a public legal action.

What this doctor did not realise (and this is a bit of free advice for all doctors, and lawyers) is that people generally do not sue people they like. Explaining to a patient what has happened and why, and expressing regret without admitting liability (which would upset the insurance company) is a good way to avoid legal action. Not only that, it seems to me that it is the right thing to do.

I've lost count of the number of clients I saw during those early years who only wanted to understand what had happened. I would warn them that they didn't necessarily have any sort of legal action available to them but we wouldn't know until we fully investigated the situation. Without exception, whenever I had to tell a client after a few months of work that what had happened to him or her in the course of their medical treatment was just one of the intrinsic risks of their treatment, which could occur without any negligence at all on the part of the doctor, they were grateful, and only wished they had been told earlier.

Other medical negligence clients had a more altruistic motive: they wanted to make sure that what happened to them did not happen to anybody else. Again, an apology and an assurance that a lesson had been learnt would have gone a long way in these situations. I felt dreadful taking people's money to find out what they should have been told anyway, and spent a lot of time running around giving lectures trying to 'change the world' and encouraging doctors to be more forthcoming. I hope that I achieved at least a modicum of success.

During my time working in medical negligence with my first employers, I wrote and had published a book about 'informed consent'. Informed consent involves doctors telling patients what their treatment involves, including the alternatives and risks. As part of the publicity for the book I gave a number of radio and newspaper interviews. It was then I learnt about the need to make clear to the media what is off the record.

A journalist had been chatting with me about what I had done before I became a lawyer. Among other things I had been a childbirth educator and I flippantly (and stupidly) explained a theory to her about encouraging breech babies to turn before birth by getting the expectant mother to stand on her head. The next day's newspaper carried this as a story. I don't think I was very popular with my boss that day.

Around this time I was also invited to speak at a number of medical meetings and conferences about how to avoid getting sued. The drug companies are not permitted to overtly bribe doctors to prescribe their drugs, but they certainly know how to turn on some good food and wine at the conferences!

The publicity from my book did not endear me to some of my colleagues. I was a new lawyer from out of town and had suddenly become highly visible. There were a number of complaints made to my employers about the fact that I was being perceived as a specialist in the field of medical negligence. One of the strange things about the legal profession is that whether you are an expert in a particular area or not, you are generally not allowed to say so publicly, or let the media present you in this light.

The rule has its roots in the desire of lawyers not to descend into the grotty world of touting and undignified, sensationalist advertising, but one of its effects to make it very hard for members of the public to find out which lawyers do what sort of work and just who is any good at their job. As with any job, there are more and less able lawyers, and this rule allows the mediocre and barely competent to survive and prosper.

Me being me, I let this criticism hurt me. I couldn't understand why people had a problem with me talking about a subject I knew something about, in public. Me also being me, I kept on doing what I was doing anyway.

Medical Victims

The medical negligence case files were filled with strange and sad stories.

One of my clients was a delightful lady in her late sixties. She had been admitted to hospital for a colonoscopy as she had been having some bleeding from the bowel. A colonoscopy is a look up a person's (how do I put this nicely?) 'bottom' with a little lighted telescopey sort of thing. Colonoscopies are often done under sedation but sometimes under a light general anaesthetic. When she woke up from the general anaesthetic, she found that she had received grommets in both her ears. Grommets are the little tubes they put in the ears of young children who are prone to middle ear infections. One would have thought that the surgeon would have at least double-checked that he was operating on the right person when he found someone of her age apparently waiting for this operation. I am still searching for the child who went in to have the grommets!

A much sadder case was that of a gentleman, also in his late sixties, recently retired from a job as an engineer, who went into hospital for day surgery to have some polyps removed from his nose to try to reduce his snoring. He was discharged that evening leaking a clear fluid from his nose. He seemed a little bit vague to his daughter, who picked him up, but she was assured that what he had was 'post anaesthetic confusion'. The next day he was very unwell and she returned him to the hospital.

It was eventually discovered that the junior surgeon who'd carried out the polyp operation had somehow, and it would have taken quite an effort, managed to get the forceps right up through the top of the nose, then through the cribiform plate (a sieve-like bony barrier between the nasal cavity and the brain), and had given my client a lobotomy, with the forceps penetrating into the right ventricle of the brain. The clear fluid leaking from his nose was cerebro-spinal fluid, which normally surrounds the brain and spinal cord.

One of the effects of a lobotomy involves a sort of dulling of the emotions. My client changed from a very mentally and physically active man to a person who was lethargic, and almost zombie-like. He said he knew, intellectually, that he should feel angry about what had been done to him, but he had somehow lost the ability to feel anger due to the damage to his brain. The really sad part, however, was that his damages for 'pain and suffering' were reduced because he wasn't suffering as much as someone who retained the ability to feel emotions to the full.

Because of my interest in patients' rights—and in particular their right to be informed about the risks of medical treatment—I had the honour to meet and become friends with a woman I think of as Australia's Erin Brockovich. (Erin Brockovich was a law clerk in the US who, despite her lack of a formal law education, was the driving force behind a successful case against the Pacific Gas and Electric Company in 1993, which proved that the company had knowingly contaminated drinking water with a toxic and carcinogenic chemical. A movie starring Julia Roberts was made about her achievements.)

Australia's Erin Brockovich is Maree Whitaker, who was blinded as a result of surgery. She was already blind in one eye as a result of a childhood accident (her brother had poked a stick into it), and a doctor had offered to improve the cosmetic appearance of that eye. Maree was a trained nurse who asked many questions about the procedure, but was not told about the very small risk of a condition known as sympathetic ophthalmia developing, which could cause her 'good' eye to stop working. This happened, and she sued. She won her case. The doctor appealed. He won the appeal.

Maree went to the High Court and won again. She was awarded damages, and the taxman then put his hand out for tax on the interest on the damages which had accrued during the appeals process. Off she went to the High Court again, and won again. What a woman. A lesser person might have given up at any of the hurdles and no-one would have blamed her. Not Maree.

The evening I met her, she was giving a speech, having been given an award by the Australian Plaintiff Lawyers Association. I had never seen her before, but met her in the foyer outside the hall where the honours dinner was being held. I did not know she was a guest of honour, but went up to her and admired the vibrant turquoise colour of her dress, saying how similar it was to the colour of the shirt I was wearing at the time. I have never been known for being particularly observant, and had completely missed the fact that she was wearing great big dark glasses—any mug would have realised that she was blind.

Despite the fact that I had well and truly put my foot in it, she and her husband Norm took an instant liking to me, and I to them. They asked me if I wanted to sit at their table. I still didn't know she was the guest of honour, so I agreed. The next thing I knew they had the gall to complain to the organisers that somebody had messed up the seating and that their very good friend Judith Fordham, who was supposed to be sitting at the head table with them, had been left out. The organisers were very apologetic and I ended up seated next to the guest of honour. I had the decency to be a little bit embarrassed.

Maree is a phenomenally brave and tenacious woman. She also has a delightfully warped sense of humour. In her speech she recounted how she had been a good-looking woman, often likened to Shirley MacLaine. Having been blind for some years, she asked a friend, 'Tell me how I look. Do I still look like Shirley MacLaine?' She had put on a little weight, and the friend blithely replied, 'No, more like Benny Hill.'

Maree told me how, despite her blindness, she continued to look after her grandchildren from time to time. She was bathing one little chap who kept crying inconsolably no matter what she did to try to pacify him. The water temperature was fine; she had checked it again and again. She couldn't work out what could possibly be going wrong. When her daughter returned home all was revealed, so to speak: she had been bathing her grandson in the pitch dark. She didn't know the difference, but he certainly did and was not impressed.

Crime does not pay

After a couple of years I started my own law firm, eventually employing several other lawyers and staff. In retrospect, I think I was far too inexperienced, but at least I had some maturity in years and avoided some mistakes because of that. I did not get as hard a time as other baby lawyers because I looked my age and so was not always picked out and picked on as a newcomer. When I opened my mouth in court I was pleasantly surprised to find that usually something sensible sounding would blurt out. As long as no-one analysed my utterances too closely I was all right.

I have to admit, I still feel that way in court quite often. I think of everyone else as a grown-up, and wonder when they are going to realise that I have strayed into the big kids' playground. Then, with my habit of over-analysing everything, I think, 'Well, if I've managed to fool so many people for such a long time, maybe I really do know what I'm doing!'

The more trials I did, the more I learnt. The more I learnt, the more I became aware of how little I knew. I wondered how on earth I could possibly have been let loose on the unsuspecting public in past years. Graduating in law was all very well, but there are countless tricks and traps I was not taught at university, and they do not hand out common sense with law degrees.

Other lawyers in my early days were often too interested in their own personal survival in court to bother with helping a new lawyer. There were some exceptions. There are still people I can telephone to ask really dumb questions of without feeling awkward. I try to remember my early experiences when I am dealing with baby lawyers and always give out advice as freely as I have time to.

At the time I started in the legal profession, there were very few women with substantial practices in criminal law. I learnt to 'mix it with the boys' in terms of dealing with police, my colleagues and, of course, my clients. Most criminals are men. This either means that men commit more crimes, or that women are smarter and don't get caught. Either way it is a compliment to women.

People will sometimes say to me, 'You defence lawyers have obviously not experienced crime.' Just because I make a living from defence work does not mean that I do not have enormous sympathy for victims. I have been a victim of violent, frightening crime several times (that is not counting what my ex-husband did to me), as have other members of my family. I do care, but I have ended up mainly defending. People who are accused of crimes should be represented, just as the interests of the State are represented by the prosecution. If accused people have an articulate voice, and some resources at their disposal, they have a chance of getting a fair go. I challenge any Australian to say that someone does not deserve a fair go.

Criminal law is certainly not the place to make a fortune as a lawyer. Commercial law, taxation law, virtually any type of law other than crime, is far more lucrative. Crime truly does not pay, even for lawyers. However, criminal law is what most people think of when they think of lawyers. The TV crime dramas and popular novels reinforce that image, and I have enjoyed being part of it. Criminal trials are not generally as dramatic as they seem on television, but they do have their amazing moments.

Criminal practice is unpredictable. You never know who or what is going to walk in the door next. The rest of this book shares some of the extraordinary experiences I have had as a criminal lawyer over the last 20 years or so.

The Flying Lawyer and Other Stories

Back at law school the thought of running my very own firm was rather glamorous. I would dream and plan whenever I was bored (which was often: most law school lectures could be bought by drug companies and their essential ingredient extracted and patented for a foolproof sleeping pill).

In my dreams I had visions of running very important meetings, wearing perfect designer clothes and floating into court wowing the judges and the assembled acolytes with my utter brilliance. I would have delightful lunches and dinners throughout which I would drink martinis but never get drunk. My make-up would be perfect, my companions handsome, my staff loyal, supportive but quirky and my sex life vigorous! Occasionally, at the end of a hard-fought trial, when all looked lost, the doors of the court would fly open at the last possible moment, a messenger would hand me a note and the real killer would be unmasked by my cunning and after-hours detective work. Sometimes the judge or the prosecutor would break down and confess that they were the real killer—perhaps being the evil twin of the accused and having been separated at birth, or …

I suppose I had been watching too much television. Running a law firm was like running any other small business. The boss was paid last, if there was anything left after paying the employees. The boss was also responsible for the quality of the product and if the customers were not happy the buck stopped with them. There was always some crisis which stopped me getting home at a civilised hour: an employee having a hissy fit, an urgent call from a client who needed something by the next morning, an insurance claim, or paperwork for the taxman.

I lost count of the number of times I worked all night. In fact I have learnt over the years that there is no point going to bed at 4.30am, only to lie there thinking, 'If I hurry up and go to sleep I can fit in two hours before I have to get up, no, make that one hour 59 minutes … I have to hurry up and get to sleep or I will run out of time to sleep … what was that I should have written down before I went to bed? Will I remember it if I try really hard or should I get up and write it down? But that means I will get even less sleep, so maybe I'll just try to remember …' If this happens now I realise that the adrenaline and caffeine coursing through my body mean that I will never get any sleep so I give up and get up. These days I know to skip the stress session in bed.

It wasn't all misery and stress, however. There were some fun times. One of the highlights of the early years was going to the northwest of the state 'on circuit'. This meant that the court would travel to isolated areas where the population was so low that a full-time court could not be provided and yet a seemingly disproportionate number of violent or drug-related crimes were committed. I always felt just a bit special flying around in a light plane as a very minor part of the justice system. I think in my fantasy world I imagined a similarity with the Royal Flying Doctor Service.

Some of the usual barriers between the judiciary, the prosecution and the defence were set aside on circuit. We would often travel to the venue of the trial on the same small scary aeroplane, all stay in the only decent pub (or more correctly the only pub) in town, and share the same menu in the same dining room or café at night. The wheels of justice were greased very effectively (and with absolute propriety) in such circumstances as everybody was forced to talk to each other and the thing we had most in common was the case we were all involved in. I am thrilled to see our brand spanking new Chief Justice has now introduced in the city something called 'criminal case mediation' where the parties get together with a neutral third party and see what they can agree on. Sometimes a trial might be avoided by coming to some civilised, mutually acceptable compromise. Clearly someone has told him how things used to get sorted out on circuit. The only thing he needs to introduce in the citified version is a few beers and I am sure things would go just as well as they did in the country.

One circuit case involved flying to a small town for a two-day trial. A truck had rolled after an accident. Since the truck contained an assortment of wine, golf clubs, stereo systems and other desirables, rather than rusted machinery and sheep manure, the townsfolk had descended like a flock of seagulls around abandoned fish and chips. Most of the locals had decided that international maritime salvage laws applied and that finders were definitely keepers. My client was not quick enough, and was still at the scene helping himself from the back of the truck when the local constabulary arrived. He was apprehended and charged. I always wondered if the real reason he was charged was because he and others had beaten the police to the loot, but that would be an unkind and uncharitable thought.

The first and worst thing about this and other trips in light planes was having to be weighed before I was allowed to get on the plane. As if my extra piece of chocolate the night before was going to make this miracle of engineering drop out of the sky! I was used to flying on large aeroplanes where the reality of being heavier than air had always mercifully escaped me. This business about having to walk across the tarmac and clamber up a set of three or four steps into a sardine tin, rather than walk through a carpeted tube into a large aeroplane, was confronting for a sheltered city girl like me. And to have to hand one's luggage over to the pilot who doubled as a baggage handler and watch him put it in the nose of the plane where I thought the engine should be, was seriously scary. What sort of pilot could he be, if he had to handle people's bags? Did he fail Real Pilot School and have to practise on disposable people

On this trip I sat next to the police prosecutor. During the flight, we went through all the evidence and agreed between us which witnesses needed to be called and which witnesses didn't. The two-day trial was over in half a day. One of the relatively minor charges was dismissed because we had dispensed with so many witnesses that there wasn't enough evidence any more, and my client was found not guilty on some and guilty on other charges. No-one especially cared, except the client.

After a pleasant afternoon killing time with the prosecutor and the police witnesses, we all repaired to the local pub and found the magistrate had beaten us to it. Looking up from his beer, his comment was, 'Next time you two are going to set me up, do you think you could let me know first?'

Lost wallets and rocket launchers

Some planes were a little bigger, but they had their own hazards, such as the food. (The small ones only had biscuits and thermos coffee if you were lucky.) I learnt early in my flying lawyer career not to overindulge in the demon drink the night before such a flight. The worst feeling in the known universe must be sitting in a very cramped flying cigar, head cocked to one side to avoid hitting the wall of the plane, suffering from a hangover. On a trip to the North West I had to set the alarm for 4am to catch the plane. I was just starting to relax, feeling a bit queasy but not too bad, when breakfast was handed out. Imagine a plane full of people simultaneously peeling the foil off their reconstituted eggs and anaemic pork sausages and bacon, all swimming in the clear liquid leached from the fried tomato. The smell was stomach-turning. Never again.

On that trip, I was travelling to Karratha, a mining town some hours' flight from Perth. There was no such thing as a typical trip to Karratha. Every one was an adventure.

My first task, once my stomach had settled, was to advise and appear in court for a client who had lost her wallet. One doesn't normally have to appear in court when one has lost a wallet. One normally cancels credit cards, hopes to get the wallet back and generally gets on with life. However, this particular wallet contained a small quantity of amphetamines. The sensible course for my client to have taken would have been to buy a new wallet. But no, this clever young lady reported it missing.

It was eventually handed in, complete with money and drugs. Of all the times to strike an honest member of the public! The local police, once they stopped laughing, called my client to tell her that her wallet had been handed in, and then sat back and waited for her to come to them. When she arrived to retrieve her lost property, they promptly charged her with possession of amphetamines.

She told me that the police must have planted the drugs in her wallet. Being a very serious and quite naive new criminal lawyer at the time, I went to see the local Detective Sergeant and accused him and his colleague (very nicely) of planting drugs in my client's wallet. Once they had picked themselves up off the floor and got their hysterics under control, we developed some sort of mutual respect and eventually became the best of friends.

We became such great mates that on later trips to Karratha I would spend the morning in court and, as there were no flights back till the following day, these same drug-planting detectives would entertain me for the afternoon. With them as my tour guides, I took four-wheel-drive trips to vibrant green oases in the midst of the ochre red Pilbara soil and boat trips to islands anchored in the blindingly turquoise water.

One of these detectives, after he moved back to Perth, would take my children to karate lessons from time to time. Such kindness was hugely appreciated by this busy single-parent lawyer and her children. I would repay the favour from time to time. When they had an investigation which raised some difficult legal question, the detectives would telephone me and run the question past me. I was more than happy to help, so long as it wasn't one of my clients in the firing line. I will always treasure my memories of the real Australian outback and the good-natured approach of these men.

On this same first visit to Karratha, I represented a creative customer who had been apprehended at a roadhouse on his way towards the Western Australia/Northern Territory border carrying an AK47 and a rocket launcher, as well as an enormous quantity of ammunition. An AK47 is a Soviet-made semi-automatic assault rifle designed by one Mikhail Kalashnikov in 1947, hence its name: *Avtomat Kalashnikova 1947*. It is capable, so Wikipedia tells me, of firing 600 rounds a minute. These weapons are illegal in Australia unless you have a collector's licence; the gun is disabled by having the barrel filled in and the mechanism welded up. The less said about the rocket launcher the better. When pulled over by police, his reason for carrying the weapons, he claimed, was that he was going kangaroo shooting. They must have been very well-armed, large and dangerous kangaroos to require that arsenal. It is really hard to give such ridiculous excuses to the magistrate, even if your client insists they are the truth, especially when all those around you are rolling on the floor laughing. For some reason people spent a lot of time laughing at me in Karratha.

Work in Karratha finished, the question was how to get back home. A pilots' strike had started while I was away from Perth. All flights on the commercial airlines were cancelled. There were no rental cars to be had, and in any case it was an enormous drive even by Australian standards. My newfound evil drug-planting detective friends came to the rescue. They managed to score me a seat on the plane that delivered the newspapers by air every day.

It was a 12-seater Beechcraft King Air. I managed to secure the last remaining seat, which was the co-pilot's seat. I had never flown in a co-pilot position before and I certainly did not know how to fly a plane. I couldn't see ahead. My seat was so low that I could not see over the nose of the plane. This was very disconcerting. It didn't seem to worry the pilot, who was taking more notice of his instruments than of what he could see ahead.

I really wanted to be able to see where I was going, however, so I asked the pilot what to do. He told me to move a lever and push my feet against the floor and my seat would lift up. I found the lever, but in order to push my feet I needed something to hang onto. There were some convenient handles in front of me so I grabbed them, pulled with all my might and got the seat up. The nose of the plane headed almost vertically upwards. Well, how was I to know that the co-pilot controls had not been turned off? It certainly woke up everyone dozing in the back of the plane.

After that, I was placed on flight attendant duties. This involved reaching under my seat for a thermos of coffee and a box of motel style mini-packs of biscuits, and passing them to the passengers behind me. At least I did not mess that up.

We had to stop in Paraburdoo to drop off some more newspapers and to refuel. I had never been there, but had heard people in the northwest call it 'Para–bloody–burdoo'. That was all I knew of the place. All I could see as we landed was tarmac and terminal. For all I knew that was all there was.

The pilot and passengers climbed down the rickety steps from the plane and walked across the shimmering tarmac to the terminal, which was a hut with a small patch of lawn in front of it, a low fence and a couple of shrubs. The aggressive heat sucked the moisture out of my lungs. The temperature would have been about

44 degrees Celsius, but it was far hotter standing in the radiant heat of the tarmac.

Refuelling was very much like what happens at the local service station. While all the passengers stood in the ribbon of shade on the ochre-stained concrete slabs outside the terminal building, we watched the pilot wrestle a hose from a reel and place the nozzle in a hole on the wing. As we watched, a reddish brown dog (roughly the same colour as the expanse of red soil which stretched as far as the eye could see) skittered across the tarmac, raced up the stairs to the plane and appeared a moment later with a little brown bag in his jaws. He raced back down the stairs and headed for the drought-resistant shrubs. Flippantly, I said to someone wilting next to me, 'I hope that wasn't the pilot's lunch.'

Refuelling completed, we took off. I kept my hands off the handle thingies in front of me. Once at very low cruising altitude, the pilot started reaching under his seat. I took my headphones off (as I hadn't worked out how to talk to him with them on) and asked, 'Are you looking for something?'

'Yes,' he said, 'the wife made me some ham and cheese sandwiches this morning and I can't find them.' I am not sure my laughter was appreciated.

'This is Kalgoorlie.'

Another town I flew to on circuit from time to time was Kalgoorlie. Kalgoorlie is a goldmining town. The locals have a fairly robust attitude to life. There is open prostitution at the many brothels in the town. Barmaids used to and sometimes still do lift their tops and flash their breasts for a fee. It used to be twenty cents but I suspect with inflation (money, not breasts) it is more these days. It is known as a hard drinking town. There is a special gold stealing squad—not to steal gold, as the name would suggest, but to detect the stealing of gold, a fairly common occupation in town. It is said that it is near impossible to get a conviction for gold stealing in Kalgoorlie as the local juries see it as a legitimate activity, much like taking paper clips and ballpoint pens home from the office.

It was a Monday morning, day one of the trial. My client had been charged with assault occasioning grievous bodily harm. He had hit someone with a plank of wood, fracturing his victim's skull and causing minor brain damage. It was always going to be an interesting trial, as neither he nor his victim had any recollection of the incident, and all the witnesses were drunk at the time.

I sat waiting at the long desk (the bar table) in the courtroom for the trial to begin. The heat was oppressive. The fans wobbled and squeaked overhead. 'Those ceiling fans need a wheel balance, WD40 or whatever ceiling fans get,' I thought, 'and I really wish someone would get rid of that wasp's nest in the corner of the ceiling.' A police officer approached me, 'Ms Fordham, do you know where your client is?'

'No, I haven't seen him today. Why, hasn't he turned up?'

It seemed he had indeed not turned up, and the trial was due to begin in a matter of minutes. Several police went off to search for him. About half past ten, half an hour after the usual start time, he was dragged in. I say dragged because he was obviously incapable of walking. He had an officer supporting him on either side, his clothes were filthy, he wore no shoes and reeked of cheap wine, more than likely cask Moselle. He was deposited in the dock and promptly passed out. The police told me they had found him asleep under the railway bridge after what was probably a week on a liquid diet.

'All rise!' was the call from the usher, and the judge entered. After various housekeeping matters had been attended to, I stood up and asked for an adjournment of the trial.

'What possible reason could you have to seek an adjournment of this trial at this late stage?' demanded the judge.

'Well, your Honour, my client seems to be unconscious.'

'So?' (Or judicial words to that effect.)

'Your Honour, I have not come prepared with case law or a written argument to support what I'm saying, but I did think there was some sort of law saying that the accused is supposed to be conscious and able to follow what is going on in court.'

'Ms Fordham, you are altogether too precious. This is Kalgoorlie. We are in the bush. He will sober up as the day goes on and you can tell him what happened afterwards.'

In the end, after I had nagged and nagged, the judge, clearly unimpressed, reluctantly held the matter over to the next day. The next day I went to see my client, who was being held in a cell at the local police station. He had the DTs now, didn't he? He was hallucinating: feeling giant ants crawling out of his skin and seeing things that were not there. I got a doctor in to see him and the doctor told me what I already suspected: my client was not fit to stand trial.

Back to court. Quaking in my high heels, I asked for another adjournment. The judge was not prepared to accept a medical certificate to prove my client was not fit for trial. He insisted on seeing the doctor in person.

'But your Honour, the doctor does not want to come to court. He has examined my client and written a detailed report which your Honour has.'

'If the good doctor does not choose to grace the court with his presence, I will have him arrested,' said his Honour. He probably had no power to carry out the threat, but it had me worried.

I got on the phone and begged the doctor to come in, which he reluctantly did. Even more reluctantly, the judge granted an adjournment. His time on circuit in the town did not allow for the trial to be rescheduled for the later that particular trip, so the judge remanded my client in custody for about three months until the next circuit sittings.

I'm not sure whether it was a death wish or a warped sense of humour, but my parting shot was to say to his Honour: 'I suppose bail is out of the question?' I didn't seriously think I would get a reply, and I didn't, unless you count a loud snort.

Feeling Superstitious

Not only have judges frequently failed to appreciate my amazing intelligence, wit, knowledge, magnetic personality and savoir faire, but my clients have often failed dismally too. In another northwest town, Port Hedland, I was asked for legal advice by a chap who was charged with a serious drug offence: cultivating a substantial hydroponic crop of cannabis and planning to sell it. He pleaded not guilty, and the case eventually came to trial. Whether he lacked some confidence in our criminal justice system or not was not clear—it may just have been his Eastern European village upbringing. Whatever it was, he decided to take out some 'special insurance' to ensure his speedy acquittal.

I met him at court and escorted him to the detention area where he was required to 'check in' before the trial.

In the middle of the corridor, he suddenly stopped dead in his tracks, turned and sat down. He looked up at me. 'Are you superstitious?' he asked.

'Not particularly,' was my reply.

He fossicked in the pocket of his waistcoat and produced two rolled up paper tissues. ('Oh, goody,' I thought, 'another "special" client.')

'An old lady gave me this yesterday. She told me how to win this case,' he said. He unwrapped one of the tissues and from it produced two neatly peeled cloves of garlic, with which he proceeded to draw a cross on the sole of each shoe. I was somewhat taken aback. He then unwrapped the other tissue, which he told me contained a mixture of salt and sugar. 'I'm going to sprinkle this in a circle around my seat in the dock,' he announced. He knew, from past experience, that he would not be permitted to take items of personal property through the detention system with him and into court so he handed the tissue to me and asked me to give it to him when we met up again in the courtroom. The thought of handing a client a rolled up tissue of white powder in court did not appeal to me one little bit so I refused.

As the trial began, one after the other the prosecution witnesses fail to implicate him. By 3pm on that day, I confidently made an application to the judge to direct the jury to deliver a verdict of not guilty, on the grounds that there was no case at all for this client to answer; that is, there was no evidence at all on which the jury could convict him. By 4pm he was a free man.

He was joined by a number of his compatriots and the group retired to a local hotel. I was persuaded to join in. After all, it seemed a natural thing to do after such a stupendous victory. The client came up to me, and I readied myself for a suitably self-deprecating response to the fulsome praise which was about to be bestowed upon me for my efforts. He was glowing: 'See, I told you that garlic would work.'

I thought about carrying a supply of garlic, salt and sugar for future trials when all other avenues failed, but decided that that was going beyond the call of duty. If I started doing that, I was also going to have to carry lucky rabbits' feet, shrunken heads and all manner of potions and charms, depending on the client's particular beliefs. I'm sure that even if I did not fall foul of the Bar Rules (the rules of ethical behaviour for barristers), I would certainly have fallen foul of the Health Act. We couldn't have that.

My Life of Crime

Despite all the valuable experience I gained on circuit, it still didn't take much to shake my fragile self-confidence. Since childhood, I had always fretted about the mistakes I made, and seen my successes as more good luck than good management. My first school report at four years of age read, 'Judy is a worrier.' I haven't changed. I still wonder, to this day, when people are going to realise that I'm just faking it and that I don't really know what I'm doing. Then I think if I am such a good fake maybe I really do know what I'm doing. Something inside keeps me on my toes and makes me try constantly to achieve: probably the sense of not being good enough that my father instilled in me and reinforced over the years.

One young bank robber showed a real lack of faith in my abilities. He had been on bail waiting for his time in court. He had always intended to plead guilty and this court appearance was to get him sentenced. The only question was how long he would spend in gaol. Having been on bail, he came to court voluntarily, handed himself in to the custody officer and took his place in the dock. He pleaded guilty as expected and sat back to listen to me give a YSS speech.

'YSS' was a term often used in our little criminal law practice to describe a young client who had fallen foul of the law for no apparent reason, had nothing particular to recommend him (and it was almost inevitably a 'him'), and who was as guilty as sin. In these situations, something had to be said to the magistrate or judge to get the best deal we could on a sentence. The theory was that if all else failed, one could always fall back on YSS: 'Young, Stupid and Sorry'. Strangely, most clients would be willing to hear themselves called 'stupid', but some really choked on the concept of 'sorry'. I guess it shows just how stupid some of them really were!

In this instance, I had been rabbiting on for quite some time when the judge decided a tea break was called for. Court adjourned, and my bank robber was taken down the rickety wooden steps to the holding cells beneath the courtroom. (I thought of these cells as a dungeon: a concrete bear pit surrounded by barbed wire, fiercely hot in summer and icy in winter. A horrid place to be locked up in.)

About 20 minutes later, we all reassembled in the wood-panelled courtroom. Lawyers sat at the red-topped bar table, on fiendishly uncomfortable but very impressive red seats with wrought iron sides. Dust particles danced in a ray of sunshine from the windows high up on a wall above the paintings of old judges and historical scenes. The lion and the unicorn held their brightly coloured shield on the wall above and behind the judge. My client and his co-accused were in the dock, a platform about a metre above the ground surrounded by an ornate wooden railing about a metre high. We sat quietly, shuffling papers and waiting for the judge to make his grand entrance, preceded by his usher loudly commanding us to 'All rise!'

Before this ritual could take place, however, all hell broke loose behind us: loud crashing and banging, shouts and curses. I turned just in time to see my client vaulting over the edge of the dock and running out the door of the courtroom, hotly pursued by guards. I am told that he ran all the way to St Georges Terrace, some hundreds of metres away. He then tried to hijack a car, but was swiftly apprehended.

There are two things that I have puzzled over ever since: first, was my representation of him really so bad that he had to run away halfway through it? Second, if he was going to run away, why on earth didn't he do it while he was still on bail, rather than waiting till he was in the courtroom surrounded by guards?

Gobbledygook!

Appearing in the High Court of Australia is not a particularly enjoyable experience. I think it takes a very peculiar and masochistic person to genuinely enjoy that jurisdiction, which perhaps explains why so many lawyers seem to enjoy it. I had never appeared in the High Court before when the Court came from the nation's capital to Perth, rather like the courts in Perth go on circuit in remote areas of our state. No doubt for the High Court judges, all based in the eastern states, Perth was very much the back of Bourke.

I was appearing in court *pro bono*, that is for free, to argue that my client's wilful murder conviction should be overturned. It was a fairly subtle argument about whether or not the judge had correctly instructed the jury about how they should go about their task. My argument must have been very subtle because one of the High Court judges announced, 'Ms Fordham, this is all meaningless. It's gobbledygook!' This comment did nothing for my self-confidence. After all, if I was not being understood by a High Court judge, I must indeed have been speaking gobbledygook.

I was so nervous that my tongue was sticking to the roof of my mouth. I tried to pour myself some water. That was a real trap for a new player. Being in the exalted jurisdiction of the High Court, instead of the plastic jugs and disposable cups that I was accustomed to in other courts, there was a glass jug with water and ice and a real glass. Try not making a noise and not spilling anything when your hands are shaking violently. I gave up and soldiered along with my tongue still firmly stuck to the roof of my mouth.

I knew I had a time limit of 20 minutes to make my argument. I also knew that the judges would interrupt and ask questions from time to time. What I had not counted on was just how many questions, how long it would take to answer them, and how fast my allotted time would slip away … without me having said anything from the list of stunning things I had planned to say. The worst, most disconcerting and cruellest thing of all was a contraption like a set of traffic lights on the associate's desk between the judges and the place I was standing. When I had five minutes to go the lights started flashing amber and when my time was up I knew they were going to turn red. I felt like a kangaroo hypnotised by the headlights of an oncoming road train.

As a reminder of that experience, I kept the 'gobbledygook' section of the transcript, enlarged it and framed it. It lives on my office wall. I look at it when I want to feel sick, but really to remind me never to put myself in that position again. I actually succeeded in that application to the High Court, so I can now say I have a 100 per cent success record there and I do not plan to spoil that record by going back, ever.

Pizza theft

I enjoyed my very first appearance in a criminal court much more than the High Court experience. I treated every case very seriously, and this was no exception. My client had been charged with a series of heinous crimes, and it was all down to a ham and pineapple pizza, or at least a ham pizza.

He had ordered a home delivery pizza from a well-known chain (name suppressed). It was a Hawaiian pizza and as such, gentle reader, you will appreciate that pineapple is required as part of the topping. This pizza had no pineapple. My client complained. The delivery man poked his finger around in the pizza attempting to winkle out some shreds of pineapple in order to convince my client that he was wrong. Understandably my client then refused to pay for the pizza.

Within ten minutes, two young uniformed police officers were at his door. I suspected, although I didn't really know, that they may have received the odd discount pizza in their time. They told my client to pay up. My client refused. They grabbed him and told him he was under arrest for stealing a pizza. He objected and struggled and they then told him he was under arrest for resisting arrest. He swore at them and they then told him he was under arrest for disorderly conduct by swearing. He struggled some more and they told him he was under arrest for assaulting a police officer.

These last three charges are known in the trade as 'the trifecta', and defence lawyers will often (cynically and entirely without foundation, I am sure) allege that their client was charged with the trifecta because police had been a bit heavy-handed in their treatment of the client, and did not want to have an official complaint made about their actions. Attack is the best form of defence and all that.

After the pizza refuser was released on bail, he decided he needed some legal help. He pleaded not guilty to everything and the case went to trial. The magistrate acquitted him of everything and went on to make some rude remarks about the quality of the pizzas he himself had received from that particular chain. A newspaper reporter happened to be in court (I rather suspect the magistrate was well aware of this) and the journalist thought this trial would make the basis of an interesting little article.

The next day, on page three of the biggest newspaper in Western Australia, there was an article quoting the magistrate's comments about the quality of that particular brand of pizza. It was headed up, I think, 'The Case of the Dud Dial-a-Pizza'. It can't have done sales much good, so that just proves there is justice in our courts, doesn't it?

Police tales

The eighties were also the times of very indulgent Christmas parties. The police Christmas parties, in particular, were extraordinary. Times have changed and I am sure such parties no longer occur, but as a defence lawyer and a female, not necessarily in that order, I was astounded at the very masculine 'culture' celebrated at these events. If it wasn't rubber chickens hanging from trouser flies, it was mother and daughter topless waitress teams, risqué movies and several offers of stress relief massages at each event. These officers had a philosophy of working hard and playing hard. I had to find a way of keeping up without joining in. I could write a book about those days, and those parties, but there is and was a rule that what is said and done at these functions stays at these functions. Call it honour among thieves, if you like.

I have quite a number of police friends, despite the fact that I spend most of my working time accusing them of telling lies and arresting the wrong people. It's a credit to their professional attitude that they can see past the job to the person.

Although I never called on the friendships I had with police in any dodgy way, I was glad to be able to call on them when my children came home one day and told me that the man in the flats across the road had been asking them to come into his flat to watch videos. He would wait outside a block of flats and pick up children on their way home from school and take them inside to watch videos. My children had never gone inside but as soon as I heard about it my 'dirty old man' radar started pinging.

There was nothing really that I could report to police. Nothing had happened. I didn't know what was on the videos. I just had a strong feeling that something was wrong. I rang some officers I knew, and they took me seriously, paid the man a visit and let him know that he was being watched very, very carefully. I believe this stopped his generous offers to passing children.

There were some police, however, who I could have cheerfully strangled. Top of the list were the officers who thought it was funny to allow one of my clients, who had been picked up drink-driving at 3.30am, to make a (drunken) call to his lawyer. I did not find it in the least funny.

I also lacked a sense of humour when I sent my secretary to pick up a client's belongings from the police station after detectives had finished their inquiries, and one of the officers made a point of showing her the very small bag of green herbal material in the briefcase to be returned to my client. My secretary, who was a sweet innocent young lady, showed this to me. She told me she couldn't work out why they were laughing.

It was unquestionably cannabis. That meant first that the police officer concerned had supplied cannabis, which was a criminal offence, but also that I was now in possession of cannabis, also a criminal offence.

I rang the officer in charge of the police station and told him exactly what I thought of his junior's sense of humour. He had tried to convince me that it was only oregano. I called his bluff saying that if he wasn't at my office in ten minutes to pick the 'oregano' up, I was going to send it off to be analysed. I didn't know that police cars could travel at the speed of light, but evidently they can.

I chose not to make an official complaint as it was only someone's utterly misguided sense of humour and I didn't want to ruin his entire career. That young officer does not know how lucky he was.

Sometimes police place themselves in positions more embarrassing than illegal.

I recall the officer who was part of a drugs raid on the house of one of my clients. Part of the point of raiding a house is the surprise element, as anyone who watches television will be aware. If a drug dealer has advance warning of the police arriving, he is hardly likely to leave drugs around. A favourite way of getting rid of drugs quickly is by flushing them down the toilet. My client certainly seemed surprised when the police burst in through the front door.

He was seen leaving the lavatory, naked from the waist down. He was immediately pinned to the ground and the police officer noticed a piece of toilet paper protruding from between his rather large buttocks. (The client's buttocks, that is, not the officer's.) The officer's statement read: 'I asked the occupant what was between his buttocks, and he replied "shit". Believing "shit" to be a slang term for drugs, I removed the toilet paper. It was not drugs.' I had the distinct impression no forensic analysis was required for the officer to come to that conclusion. I wonder how long it took the observant officer to live that one down.

I have just as much sympathy for the young constable who turned up to serve a warrant for non-payment of traffic fines at a house shortly after a murder had taken place there. He was looking for my client's boyfriend, who just happened to be the murderer. He spoke to my client outside the house as she was loading things in the back of a van. He asked her where the boyfriend was. She professed to have no idea.

Having an inquiring mind, which is a good quality for a young police officer, he then pointed to a roll of carpet hanging out of the back: 'What's that in the back of the van?'

'Oh nothing, just some junk,' she replied. The so-called 'junk' actually concealed the body. I would imagine that this young man was severely embarrassed about his failure to have a look at that 'junk' more closely. Fancy having to give that evidence in court at a murder trial!

A parent's guide to interrogation

I've learnt a lot through my contact with the police over the years. You don't cross-examine detectives day in and day out and not pick up some of their investigative techniques. My children experienced the results from time to time, and they were not in the least happy about it.

I had been away with my husband (the nice one) for a few days. We left one of my children at home. She was 16. We arrived home some hours earlier than we had planned to.

I have a very acute sense of smell, and I loathe the smell of cigarettes. I think this stems from my childhood, when our annual summer holiday involved driving north for many hours in a Volkswagen Beetle, my mother and father in the front, my grandmother, myself and one sister in the back seat, and another sister in the parcel area behind the back seat. The rear windows on a Volkswagen Beetle do not wind down—there are only quarter vents. It was hot and airless. I was prone to carsickness. My mother chain-smoked all the way. I vomited all the way. When I studied psychology at university, I realised that I had experienced 'homegrown' aversion therapy sessions in the back of that car.

Back to my trusted 16-year-old. We walked up the front steps and into the house. As I walked into the house, I noticed it had an odd smell, as if someone had been smoking. There was also a waft of something else, which reminded me of standing outside a country pub—the faintest breath of beer.

All was quiet. No-one at home. As we walked through the kitchen and lounge room, the beer and cigarettes smell became stronger. Puzzled, I checked the kitchen. Attached to the refrigerator was a party invitation and a note. There were some standing rules in our household about going to parties. I insisted on seeing the invitation, knowing where the party was being held and when it was to finish. The note read, 'Hi Mum, I'm at a party. I know you like to see the invitation so here it is.' I was already suspicious. The note was out of character, and there was still this odd smell. I took the invitation off the refrigerator and had a closer look. It was handwritten on one of those tear-off party invitation pads that can be bought at most newsagents. The plot thickened. (I have always wanted to say that.) I noticed there was something missing from the invitation. There was no telephone number for an RSVP.

I put the invitation down and started my criminal investigation in earnest. I checked the rubbish bins in the kitchen. Nothing suspicious. I checked the large green wheelie bins outside. On the surface, nothing suspicious. But I hadn't spent quality time with police officers for nothing. I lifted the top layer of newspapers in the wheelie bins and there were the beer bottles. Many, many beer bottles.

I went back to the kitchen, and pulled on a pair of gloves. Not the yellowish forensic type, but nasty green washing-up gloves. They still accomplished the task of keeping my hands clean while conducting my search, and I did not think I had to be concerned about contaminating whatever I found with my own DNA. I pulled the beer bottles out of the wheelie bins, and excavated further. The next layer down included the contents of several ashtrays. Cigarette butts galore, and something which looked like roll-your-own cigarettes but were irregular and a little different in their odour.

Back to the invitation. Starting to suspect that my daughter had not spent a quiet weekend studying, and wanting to get her home immediately to find out what had been going on I went to her address book to try to find the telephone number for the party giver. As I opened the address book, a *draft* of the invitation fell out. The plot positively congealed. I found the telephone number of the girl who was (supposedly) giving the party. I rang her and inquired about the party. She wasn't quick enough. There was no party and she told me so. She didn't know where my daughter was. I worked my way through the telephone numbers of my daughter's closest friends. Not being a police officer, I was allowed to use inducements, threats and promises to secure a confession. One of the friends cracked and informed me that there had been a party at our place the previous night, and that my daughter was probably at a beach party now.

I raced to the car, wishing I had a blue light to slap on the roof and a siren, but made do with travelling significantly over the speed limit. On the way to the beach I spotted my daughter, one of her girlfriends and two unknown male persons walking along the side of the road. I pulled over, ordered the two males to disappear immediately if they knew what was good for them, and ordered the two miscreants, 'Into the car, both of you, now.' I drove off, watching carefully in the rear-view mirror.

The two girls exchanged glances. I instructed the hapless duo, 'Not a word to each other.' I knew about crooks cooking up stories and it was not going to happen on my shift. At home, the interrogation began. 'Right. One of you is going into the bedroom. The other is going to tell me what happened. I am then going to ask the first girl what happened. If your stories don't match, I will know that one or both of you are lying. And hand over your mobile phones. I don't want you contacting your friends (that is, other potential witnesses) to work out what to say.' If I hadn't been so angry I would have been enjoying this.

To their credit, or perhaps due to sheer fright, the two girls did give the same story. It had to do with meeting two young men on the beach, and inviting them back to our place for an impromptu party. The fact that they did not know the young men's surnames did not seem to concern them. Mighty stern words were spoken regarding personal safety and (not as important) the safeguarding of property. My daughter was grounded for an entire term. Again to her credit, she agreed that she deserved it.

The postscript to the story, luckily for my daughter, came after the grounding was over. We had been having trouble with rising damp, which in a relatively new house was surprising. After extensive investigations, a plumber investigated the downpipes, and hauled out a pair of men's underpants. We assumed that somehow one of the builders had left them behind but could not work out how or why. Some weeks later, we were visiting some neighbours and happened to mention the unusual find of a pair of stray underpants. The neighbours solved the mystery.

It seems that during the illicit party, the neighbours, investigating the noise, looked across at our house and noticed that there were several people on the roof. It was a balmy evening, which would explain two things: why people were outside on the roof, and why at least one gentleman found his underpants a tad hot. I threatened to tell this story at my daughter's 21st birthday party, but had mercy in the end. Whether she will ever speak to me again after this book is published remains to be seen.

I'm pretty sure she won't speak to me again when she realises that I have also mentioned her one and only drink driving exploit. She, like many young people, did not realise just how few drinks it takes to put one over the legal driving limit. She was caught and charged with drink driving and had to go to court. She was mortified and there was no way she wanted me to know about it. Having just got her first car, she suddenly went on a very rigorous health kick and announced that she was going to get the train to work in future and walk from the station in order to stay fit and save money on petrol.

She went on and on about her new healthy lifestyle. I knew something was going on, but I didn't know what. What she didn't count on was the fact that I have an enormous network of spies and informants in the justice system. Immediately after her court appearance, I had nine email messages and four telephone calls to let me know that someone with the same family surname had appeared in court on a drink driving charge. I have to say, she has been extremely careful not to drink and drive ever since, and I'm very proud of her. (I wonder whether that will be enough to get her talking to me again?)

Special thanks

The ultimate compliment for a criminal lawyer is to lose a trial for a client and have them engage you for the appeal and the retrial. These realistic and decent people would console me after a loss which would see them locked up for many years, with a 'Never mind, mate, ya did ya best', and send Christmas cards faithfully every year.

One client sent flowers every year on the date he was convicted, 'our anniversary'. Another, upon his release from gaol, asked to take me out to lunch at the local Chinese restaurant near my office. He appeared in office reception to make this request, dressed in an ill-fitting mustard-coloured suit clearly purchased from a local charity store, set off by a red and purple tie. He announced that he had got himself 'all spoofied up' for my benefit! How could I resist? I did, but I was very nice about it, and very touched.

Criminal lawyers are forever being invited to commit crimes by their clients. A very few do so. If they are caught they are punished severely by the justice system, which requires all lawyers (yes, even criminal lawyers) to uphold very high ethical standards. Looking back, I can recall a second occasion where I committed a crime, sort of accidentally (I know, that's what they all say).

No doubt, by confessing all in this book, I will be arrested and charged by one of Western Australia's fine police officers, preferably a good-looking one. I will have my fingerprints taken and have to ask my husband or one of my children to bail me out. There will be a scandal. It will make the news at least nationally and I will sell zillions of books as a result. I will be so notorious I will have to travel first class in planes to avoid the hoi polloi and the paparazzi. I can but hope.

It came about like this. I had a fairly simple trial defending a young couple charged with possession of cannabis. Rather than getting stuck into beer or Bundy, they enjoyed an evening smoke. The difficulty was that they had been charged with intending to supply the cannabis to other people. This happened because once you have over a certain relatively small weight, the law says that you have to prove you were not going to supply it to other people. They didn't have a huge amount and it was not a terribly difficult job to convince a magistrate that it was all for their own use. No little books with financial records were found, no scales, no plastic baggies.

They had paid most of my bill in advance, but as so often happened, I was not organised enough to have secured all the money 'up front'. I would find myself seriously out of pocket from time to time but never seemed to learn my lesson, falling for sob stories and earnest promises to pay.

The couple was thrilled at the outcome. They promised to have a bottle of the best French champagne delivered to my office. That was wonderful, but a small, mean, part of me wondered whether they were proposing to pay the rest of my bill as well. How was I going to ask them, without seeming petty in the face of such a delightful offer? I did my best.

With a light-hearted (completely artificial) chuckle I said, 'That would be lovely, but don't forget the biccies!' Maybe it's my age, or where I grew up, but 'biccies' in that context meant 'money'.

A couple of days later, a gift-wrapped box arrived at my office. Never having been one for delayed gratification, I immediately tore open the wrapping.

Inside was a bottle of vintage French champagne

(Bollinger RD, in fact), but also tucked in next to the neck of the bottle, wrapped in plastic wrap, were two very heavy biscuits with a sort of greenish tinge to them. I opened the wrap up, sniffed at the green lumps and nibbled at a little corner of one.

Call me naive, but at that point I just thought I was being given the product of someone's home baking. It tasted average, to say the least. In fact, it was abominable. Suddenly I realised what had happened. My request not to forget the 'biccies' had been interpreted as a suggestion that the happy couple should donate to their favourite lawyer a cannabis cookie or two.

I don't think nibbling a corner was committing a criminal offence, as I truly had no idea what it was at the time of consumption. The ghastly act I committed was not immediately dropping the evil substance on the floor of my office and running away as fast as I could. I couldn't drop it on the floor of the office. What if the cleaner found it? What if the next client found it? What if the next police officer serving documents found it? I had to get rid of it. But where? I was not used to such dilemmas.

So did this clever, worldly-wise lawyer, giver of good advice to crooks, do anything sensible? No, I wrapped the biccies back up, shoved them in my handbag and took them home. I didn't want to put them in the rubbish (what if someone found them?). I didn't want to give them to one of my children to get rid of—heaven knows what they would have done with them. I didn't want to give them to my partner to dispose of because it would have been too hard to explain. So I just put them in the freezer and promptly forgot about them. Months later I was fossicking for something at the bottom of the freezer when this little packet turned up. I remembered what it was and then did the sensible thing: wrapped it up with the potato peelings and put in the bin. That was the end of my criminal career.

More Than a Woman

My introduction to the lot of a woman in the legal profession came shortly after I arrived in Perth. I was invited, along with many others from the relatively small ranks of the legal profession, to the opening of a set of lawyers' offices. The building itself was reasonably nondescript (I have already noted that crime generally doesn't pay, even for the lawyer). The lift lobby, though, had recently been tarted up with polished stone floors, and the walls were hung with two Persian rugs which may or may not have been valuable (I was no expert)—they were behind plexiglass screens, well out of reach of the riffraff.

The lift doors opened onto an extremely crowded passageway off which a number of individual offices opened. A strong smell of beer and a haze of cigarette smoke were my first impressions. Not much different from an Australian pub, except that the beer was imported and the carpet was not sticky (yet). Clearly the air conditioning had been turned off although it was midsummer.

I arrived before 6pm, perhaps 45 minutes after the function had begun, but I suspect (this was the eighties, after all) that some had been celebrating since lunchtime. I fought my way through the crowd to the bucket of ice and poured myself a glass of something cheap and fizzy.

As I fought my way back, I could hear an annoying whining noise, somehow familiar but out of place. It seemed to be coming from somewhere near my feet. I looked down and realised that a remote-controlled model army tank was zipping in and out among the revellers. 'Strange', I thought, and kept moving.

I had met very few local lawyers by that stage, so I gravitated towards the wall, and leant against it to observe the teeming throng. There was no music, or at least I don't think there was any. I could not really tell as the volume of a couple of hundred people in a very tight space, all talking very loudly, made it impossible to hear.

Most of the women wore black skirts with black or brightly coloured jackets. Their shoulder pads were extreme and their stilettos of an impressive height. Not many wore trousers. In those days, some crusty old judges still went through the farce of not being able to 'see' a woman who appeared before them in trousers. The effect of this was that the woman would stand up in court, and attempt to say something to the judge in earnest representation of their client, and the judge would quite literally feign deafness and blindness. He would say to the other (male) lawyer, 'Mr Smith, can you hear something? There seems to be an annoying little noise coming from the other side of the court, but I can't see anyone.'

The only male equivalent to this that I've heard of was a fellow barrister who had an intense dislike of the wig we are all forced to wear. In leaving his wig off, this man would face a vigorous argument with some judges, and be treated as invisible by others.

Little did certain judges know that I had appeared in various states of undress before them. Once I broke a heel, so I simply kicked off my other shoe and appeared barefoot, hidden from sight by the bar table. Another time I wore nothing at all under my bar jacket as the country courtroom was oppressively hot. It is hard to think straight if one is red-faced and perspiring. I was younger and prettier in those days—in retrospect, I should have told my (male) opposition about my dress or lack thereof. It might have made it difficult for him to think straight. That is known in the trade as a 'forensic advantage'.

I have never been a follower of fashion, but liked to make a point by what I wore. Animal prints were very popular in the eighties. One judge took the trouble to tell me my zebra print shoes were distracting the jury—I think they were distracting him. I repeat, it was the eighties, when many crimes against good taste were committed by better women than me.

Despite my often dubious taste, I have not hesitated to provide fashion advice for clients, though not always successfully. My advice is pretty basic. Yes, you have to wear more than a singlet and stubbies if you want to be taken seriously. Get a haircut. Get a shave. Wash! (Your clothes and yourself.) Cover the tattoos with a long shirt. Remove most of the metal from your various piercings. If you are on trial for supplying hard drugs do NOT wear a shiny silver suit, and lose the ponytail and mirrored sunglasses. Most take my advice. Bikers will shave and girls cover their midriffs.

Back to the party. The men at this gathering were not

especially noticeable by their clothing, but they were loud! Some were telling their latest war stories: how they absolutely destroyed a particular witness with a brilliant cross-examination; scurrilous stories about how Judge Bloggs should be put out to pasture as he only got his job because he was some important person's nephew and was an intellectual pygmy; how another judge kept making passes at young female lawyers, and another was drinking too much.

Welcome: you have been warned

I was enjoying catching up on the latest without having to contribute, when from somewhere in my peripheral vision a dishevelled, florid-faced man of anywhere between 40 and 60, his features blurred by his consumption of alcohol, not mine, stumbled into view. He was clearly the tank's owner or at least driver, as he held the remote in his hand, and moved towards me cursing at those whose feet interrupted the progress of the symbol of his manhood, the little tank.

He placed his sweaty face perhaps five centimetres from mine and did his best to focus directly on me.

He growled, 'You're the new girl, aren't you?'

'I guess so.'

With a blast of smoky, beery breath he then roared, 'I've got one thing to say to you, and you'd better not forget it. All women are whores and I'm going to destroy your career if it's the last thing I do.'

I was speechless. 'Welcome to Perth,' I thought.

After my initial meeting with this man, I was a little nervous around him both in and out of court. I found out many months later that he was what is known in the legal profession as 'a character'. He was well known for enjoying a drink, and each afternoon could be found propping up a certain bar in a certain hotel close to the courts. It was rumoured, although I cannot say if it was true or not, that he sometimes liked a drink during the day as well. Certainly, he often dropped off to sleep, or seemed to, during a trial. The reason I say 'seemed to' is that occasionally he would rouse himself and ask a few questions. Those few questions were often extraordinarily perceptive, cutting right to the core of the case and more often than not saving the day for his client. He was and is a very good lawyer.

He was not averse to taking the odd shortcut, however.

I did a trial with Bert Jones (I had discovered his name) when he represented one of a pair of (alleged) burglars and I represented the other. There was some fancy law in the case and at one point the judge asked us to come back in a few days with some written arguments. I rang Bert the day before the next court appearance and asked how his arguments were going.

'What arguments?'

'The ones the judge told us to produce. You must have been asleep.'

'Guess I'd better get on with that, then, hadn't I?'

The next day we were back in court. I elaborated on the arguments I had produced in writing for the judge. Then it was Bert's turn. I thought Bert was asleep, as for some minutes there had been quite audible snoring.

'Mr Jones? I don't seem to have any written submissions from you.'

A rumble came from my right as Bert roused, 'Aaaarrrrgh, I'll just go along with what she reckons.' 'She' was me. I didn't know whether to be flattered or angry.

Bert and I both got what we wanted from those arguments, but Bert managed with minimum effort and maximum effect. I wish I had those skills.

Later on in the trial, as I was in the middle of some fairly convoluted argument to the judge, there was a sudden hard tugging on the side of my robe. It was Bert. He tugged again, much harder. I sat down with a thump. 'Aaaaaargh, what she says is a load of rubbish, your Honour. The real point is …' and Bert went on to make a short, incisive, powerful and very effective speech which benefited both my client and his. I couldn't be mad at him. In fact, I was starting to develop a sneaking admiration for him.

He got away with an awful lot, and judges and lawyers were extraordinarily tolerant of his behaviour.

He did overstep the mark one evening at the Annual Criminal Lawyers' Association dinner, though. These dinners are notorious 'swim throughs', awash with alcohol, so his behaviour must have been remarkable. I'm not sure what he (allegedly) did but it must have been extraordinary even by his standards. I was told that there had been some sort of scuffle or fight, and there may have been vomiting involved. However, hearsay is a notoriously dangerous thing, so these allegations are probably untrue.

He was unofficially banned from the dinner for some years after this night. I often wondered what would have happened to me if I had behaved the same way he did. I'm sure I would have been hung out to dry for unprofessional conduct, but somehow when it was Bert doing it, the behaviour was greeted with an indulgent chuckle.

As the years went on, I was seduced by the same rough charm that everyone else had fallen for. He really was a lovable rogue, with no malice behind his often appalling behaviour. When you consider that I can say that despite our initial meeting, there must be something extraordinary about the man. He never did manage to ruin my career: in fact he never even tried, and we are now good mates. I haven't dared ask him whether he still thinks (or ever thought) all women are whores. I think it best to leave that one unanswered.

The ultimate compliment

Bikers are rumoured not to treat their womenfolk especially well, but I have never experienced anything but respect from them. They are true to their word, pay their bills (best not to think too deeply about where the money comes from), are loyal to a fault, respect a hard-fought defence win, lose or draw, and will, very occasionally, pay a compliment. The chap who wrote the following did indeed pay his bill without having to be reminded. I couldn't help but smile when I received this letter, which is reproduced exactly as I received it (and I'm sure he won't mind):

> Hey Judith, … I'm sorry embarrassed and ashamed I havent been able to fix your bill up yet. I've been ducking and diving from bailliffs, fine enforcement, tax man and a couple of shady characters who all want money from me. The few things i've tried have not borne fruit yet, and relied on a couple of people and cut them alot of slack and now they gone to ground. Also lost licence for points and another sticker on vehicle. Got done at the border with a couppla eccies, couppla little bags of wizz, a few grams of pot and a pipe. Copped a fine which was good but i still real pissed off, … dunno which is worse, Murphy's law or the system's. HAHA been seeing plenty of both. When it rains it pisses down mate. … i seem to have The Smell of Death, or something because everyones trying to rip me off. All I can say is I will do what I can and you first cab off the rank when things come good. I sorry I let you down, especially after the gr8 job you did, but murphy threw the book at me.

This is the same client who has been known to unexpectedly come up behind me on a city street—with his tattoos, dark glasses, bushy beard, torn clothing and all—and give me a big hug and say, 'G'day mate, how's it goin?' I tell him it's bad for his reputation to be seen with me.

I once defended one of these gentlemen on a charge of assault occasioning bodily harm. It is often called by my clients 'occasional' bodily harm. I believe that occasional bodily harm is indeed one of the prices they pay for their lifestyle. The exact details of the case have merged and blurred over the years with all the other occasional bodily harm cases I have done and don't matter for this story anyway.

I was standing outside court 73 during a break in proceedings. Rather than sit on the mottled bench seats stained with puddles of unspeakable substances (people get very nervous while awaiting their day in court), I was leaning against one of the beige walls. One of the witnesses (also a biker) had just been cross-examined by the prosecutor. Having calmed his nerves with a smoke outside, he wandered up to me.

In legal circles the prosecutor in this case bore the nickname 'Tommy Two Dicks', because he was 'such a wanker that one wasn't enough'. He would never use a short word if a long one would do. Judges had been known to say, when reserving days for a trial, 'Oh well, if Tom is doing it we'd better reserve twice as long,' and everyone would laugh knowingly.

The biker had made an effort to dress up for court. He had trimmed his beard, he was wearing his best black jeans (so thick with grease that they could probably stand alone), he had done up his chequered shirt so that the black T-shirt underneath hardly showed, leaving the tail of the shirt out so that the belt buckle with the insignia of his club was not visible, and the sleeves rolled down so that his tattoos were largely hidden. There was a pungent smell of 'rollies' (roll-your-own cigarettes) and last night's beer, but thankfully nothing else identifiable.

'That prosecutor,' he spluttered as he flung himself down on the seat I had earlier (I figured his jeans could stand the test), 'he's a bloody woman!'

Being used to the ways of my star witness and his friends I knew immediately what he meant. However, just in case I was unsure, he elaborated: 'Bloody pussyfooting poonce, if he'd called a spade a fuckin' shovel he might have had half a chance of getting a straight answer out of me. Couldn't fight his way out of a paper bag. Talk about a girl!'

I thought I had the general idea, but in light of the way he had gone about expressing his contempt for the prosecutor, I really thought I had to strike a blow for my gender. I looked down at him and rather gently, I thought, asked him, 'Has it occurred to you that *I* am a woman?'

He looked at me as though I had gone stark raving mad. 'Nah, mate, you're not a woman. You've got balls. You're not a bloody woman!'

What could I say? 'Thanks'. (I think.) In his world, I had just been paid the most tremendous compliment and the only thing to do was to receive it gracefully. There was no point trying to make a stand for the sisterhood. He was a lost cause. Any point I tried to make wouldn't have registered. In fact, he probably would have been offended, as he had just paid me a compliment.

One of the things I had to learn as a female operating in the world of criminal law was not to get too precious about gender stereotyping and politically correct speech. It clearly hadn't occurred to this chap that my gender was relevant to anything at all. It was my competence that mattered. What feminist could argue with that? The terms in which he chose to communicate his high opinion of me were another matter, which I chose to overlook.

'The Boss'

During my time running a small firm, I received hundreds of applications for the position of articled clerk. Law students after they graduate must be employed by another lawyer for a year as an articled clerk, which is like an apprenticeship, and for another year as a restricted practitioner. Competition for these jobs is extraordinarily fierce and the system has developed whereby all applications come in at the same time so that everyone can compete on a fair basis. As a busy principal of a small law firm, once a year I had to read mountains of these applications. It was not unusual to receive three or four hundred.

I had to work out a way of culling them quickly. Anything on pink paper went in the bin immediately. Scented paper and handwritten applications went the same way. Spelling mistakes? Out. Grammatical errors? Out. Unexplained failures in undergraduate subjects? Out. This process took the pile down to perhaps eighty applications, all of which I read meticulously.

One male graduate had as part of his academic record a High Distinction in Feminist Legal Theory. I thought this was a rather unusual subject for a young man to choose to do as part of his course and so pulled his application out from the pile for a second look. This sensitive New Age guy had started his covering letter 'Dear Sir'! Whoops.

Sometimes my sense of humour deserted me in the face of the gross provocation of being ignored or condescended to purely due to my gender. Sometimes I behaved myself and sometimes I did not when this happened. I thought I behaved myself remarkably well when the photocopier salesman came to the reception desk of my firm when I was on my way out and said, 'Can I see your boss, love?'

I kept my cool and smiled sweetly, 'I am the boss.'

'No, love. I mean the real boss.'

All I did in response was to tell him that there was no way this firm was ever going to buy a photocopier from his firm. Oh, and I did write to his manager, purely as a matter of courtesy, to let him know that my decision was a direct result of his star salesman's visit. It was only polite, after all ...

I had far more women work for me than men. They were the best people for the job at the time I was interviewing. I'm very proud of the small part I had in their early careers, as they have all gone on to considerable success. We were referred to by some of the male lawyers about town in less than complimentary terms. One of the politest was 'Youse dames'. One small but curious point, however. I had always thought it was an old wives' tale, but I can now confirm that women working in the same environment will indeed synchronise their bodies. We all, administrative, secretarial and legal staff, ended up menstruating at the same time (with the exception of the men, of course, though we threatened to get them involved too).

Lady lawyer about town

As a 'lady lawyer' about town, I was sometimes asked to functions which quite important people, usually men, also attended. At one such function, a lunch, I was placed next to the Chief Justice of Tasmania. I had never met him, I was the most junior of junior lawyers, and was quite overwhelmed at being seated next to such an august personage. He was a delightful apple-cheeked gentleman, as befitted his island of origin.

What was I to say to him? It was a bit like sitting next to the Queen. I knew I had to speak to him, but had no idea what to speak about. I did the predictable, 'What do you think of the Western Australian weather, Chief Justice?' (You can't call judges by their names. That is against the rules. You have to call them by their title.) Then, 'Have you had a chance to see some of the sights?' This conversation was going nowhere. I was bored witless, and I am sure he was too.

I am Tasmanian, but there are so many jokes about Tasmanians having more than one head and showing other genetic signs of being inbred that I tended to avoid that topic of conversation with most people. This was surely the moment to make an exception. A flash of inspiration: 'By the way, Chief Justice, I am Tasmanian too!' I announced.

The great man's eyes twinkled, and he kindly said, 'Yes, I thought there was something special about you.'

Then, without stopping to think, and apparently with a desire to see my embryonic career destroyed in an instant, (this is the time to look away from the page if you do not have the stomach for scenes of horror and disaster), I said (waving both hands in the air in case he did not understand my meaning clearly enough), 'Yes, count the fingers.'

Quite often, in a tight situation, I have opened my mouth and something sensible has come out. This was not one of those times.

In the early years, I also went to lots of cocktail parties. 'Networking' was all the rage. These functions were the sort where people circulate and talk to you, while all the time gazing somewhere over your left shoulder, looking for someone more influential and important to talk to. I attended one such party with my future husband, John. There were members of the business community and politicians, canapés and chardonnay. One of the politicians knew John and wandered over to talk to him. After he had exhausted all the small talk, and could not see anyone else worth trying to impress for the moment, he turned his attention to me. I cannot do any better or worse than repeat the conversation, verbatim (with the speaker's thoughts in italics):

'Hello. What do you do?' *Get me out of here. I have finished talking to the bloke and there is nothing he can do for me. Now I have to talk to the little woman.*

'No, don't tell me, let me guess ... You're a teacher.' *She's female. What is a woman's occupation? Get me out of here, she can't do anything for me.*

Pause with no response from me. *You've got no idea, have you?*

'No, I know, don't say anything: you're a nurse ...' *Why do I always get stuck with these bloody housewives? I am flattering her suggesting she has a job at all.*

Still no response. Bigger pause. *Loser. Suffer. I'm not going to help you.*

'I work in a law firm.' *Well, maybe I'll play with him a bit.*

'I knew it, you're a secretary!' *Surely someone is going*

to come and talk to me. I'm important, after all.

'No, actually I'm a lawyer.' *I'm sick of this.*

'A **lawyer**! Who do you work for?' *Someone has to be in charge of her— she's a female, after all.*

'I work for myself.' *You fool. Now I'm angry.*

'Ah. Family law!' *She's a girl. I've got to get this bit right.*

'What makes you say that?' *Let's see you get out of this one.*

'Well ...' *Play for time.*

'I own and run my own firm. I am a defence criminal lawyer.' *I'm bored and you are a complete loser. How did you get to this position of importance, albeit now in Opposition, thankfully? I know, you have a penis. I wonder if you have any idea what a fool you have just made of yourself? No, of course not. You are not just a fool but an ignorant fool.*

This man is still in a position of political importance. The future of our state is in good hands.

Mixing business and pleasure

Mixing business with pleasure, when it involves sleeping with clients, is considered very bad form in most professions. Doctors in particular seem to get themselves in trouble from time to time by doing this, and the professional judgement of lawyers too seems to disappear entirely once their hormones start raging. I've never found my clients sexually attractive, so have never had to worry about this particular predicament. Frankly, I don't find most lawyers particularly attractive either. With certain special exceptions, most of them are pretty boring people. Criminal lawyers are a more flamboyant breed, and most of my 'exceptions' are found among their ranks.

I don't think I've ever made a pass at another lawyer (and if anyone thinks I did they were probably drunk and misunderstood me!). I am, however, frankly proud of one incident.

Jack was a lawyer I had known and liked for a very long time, but had only ever worked with once, in a trial involving a charge alleging that my client and his co-accused exported or attempted to export portions of Australia's cultural heritage, namely a whole lot of fossils. There had never been a charge under this particular legislation before, so it was a learning curve for us both. During the trial, we developed a respect for each other as lawyers and as people. Jack had a great sense of humour, and was a brave and tenacious advocate.

Jack was diagnosed with cancer, and after fighting an extended battle, it became obvious that he was terminally ill. He left work, and I visited him from time to time. I got to know him better than when we had worked together all those years ago, and I regretted not having spent more time with him previously as a friend. Aside from visits, we also kept in touch by email during his illness.

He was a very good lawyer. His clients were lucky to

have him, and if he believed in the merit of a cause he would go far beyond the call of duty in terms of the effort he put in.

The story of the face cream is typical of the imagination, talent and courage Jack often showed. A pharmacist was being prosecuted for selling creams which were not licensed under the Therapeutic Goods Act. The defence argument (trust Jack to find a loophole) was that the cream did not need to be licensed if it was a food. He offered to eat some in front of the jury (I am told he had been practising especially). The trial judge was somewhat flabbergasted, but the prosecutor saved the day by saying that if Jack ate the cream he would become a piece of evidence (known as an exhibit) and have to go into the jury room at the end of the trial, which wouldn't do at all.

A few days before his death, he sent me an email telling me that he only had a few days to live and would like to say goodbye. Could I come and visit? I went with a mutual friend, both of us with our hearts in our respective mouths. How on earth do you say the right thing to someone who is dying? How do you be 'normal'? We arrived at Jack's place and his wife showed us down the hallway towards his bedroom door. Jack's unmistakable ocker voice rang out, still remarkably strong, 'You can't come in unless you tell a joke!' A joke? Jack had to be joking! I was only a pace away from his bedroom door and had no time to think. I opened the door, and saw him lying there. I opened my mouth, still having no idea what I was going to say.

'I don't know, Jack, I've wanted to get you into bed for years, but this is not quite what I had in mind!'

I am still rather proud of myself for that one.

Off duty

Despite the fact that I have mostly practised as a defence lawyer, I have always got on well with our State Director of Public Prosecutions, Robert Cock QC. He has fought many court battles, and a personal health battle in recent years, but is unfailingly approachable and friendly. I have had several 'off-the-record' conversations with him about legal matters of mutual concern. Above all, though, he is a good sport! Why?

Once a year, there is a Bench and Bar dinner where judges and barristers get together and let their hair down (those who still have any). Judges in particular have to be careful about 'partying', as it does not fit with the reserved, pillar-of-society image they must maintain for the public to have confidence in their decisions. At these dinners, however, there is some safety in being among like people. I am not suggesting mad orgies or anything of that nature, but we do have a good time.

This particular evening I, and many others, including the DPP, had had a good time, and the evening was drawing to a close. Somehow the conversation at our table turned to men who drink champagne from women's shoes. Robert said he was not averse to doing such a thing. Now I was, and am, a bit of a shoe nut. Shoes are my drug of choice. So I offered my new, red, sparkly, definitely not smelly shoe. I didn't think for a minute he would actually do it: it was more of a dare! But he looked as if he was really going to. I had the presence of mind to get him to wait till I set someone (a barrister who is now a judge) up with my camera to capture this historic moment.

Because of the private nature of the evening, I would never have contemplated even telling anyone the photograph existed. However, to his eternal credit, Robert has given me permission to use the photograph in this book. So there you have it, the head defender of truth, justice, and the Western Australian way of life very definitely off duty.

He Fell on the Knife

Feet up on my desk, I gazed out of my office window looking for inspiration. There was a shimmering in the air which told me it was still stinking hot, even thought it was 6pm. The traffic was unusually light, the phones had stopped ringing, and anyone with any sense had left the city early to hit the beaches and cool down. I decided I would clear two more things from my in-tray and then leave, not for the beaches but for a cold glass of champagne and a good book: my favourite way(s) of relaxing.

At that moment, Ingrid, my secretary, buzzed me. 'Judith, there's a new client here—walked straight in off the street. I said that you were just about to go home.' She lowered her voice. 'I think you should see this one. She seems like, or it seems like, your sort of client.'

Intrigued, I swung my feet off the desk and raked my fingers through my curls, straightened my skirt and slipped my not very sensible but desirable shoes back on. 'OK, show her in.' I wondered what, in my secretary's eyes, 'my sort of client' was supposed to be. Ingrid had a few strange ideas about me. She vacillated between being somewhat patronising to my face, and mocking me when she thought I wasn't paying attention. But at 100 words a minute with 98 per cent accuracy I could ignore such minor irritations. In fact, she was a huge asset to me despite her foibles, and I trusted her judgement that this would be an interesting meeting.

A tap on the door. When I looked up I was greeted by the sight of my diminutive secretary with a person who

He Fell on the Knife

was about 195 centimetres tall, square-jawed and broad-shouldered, dressed in shapeless, dusky green tracksuit pants, topped by a fluorescent orange T-shirt which bore the logo 'ALL CLASS'. 'This is Doreen,' announced Ingrid with a twitch at the corner of her mouth. 'I'm off now, unless you need me for anything else tonight?'

Doreen lumbered into the room and perched on the edge of my visitor's chair, crossing her legs at the ankle and folding her large hands over her knee to show off fluorescent pink nail polish, chipped at the edges. I suppose the saving grace was that her horny toenails were not also painted, though the white Birkenstocks she wore did nothing for the look of her feet. Doreen was quite clearly genetically male, about 50 years of age, and just as clearly making a very unsuccessful attempt to dress as a woman. I told Ingrid that all was well and she could leave. Sometimes I got a little nervous alone in my office with a new client, but despite her size, Doreen did not strike me as a threat.

I use the words 'she' and 'her' because it rapidly became obvious that this client was the latest in a long string of transsexuals who had found their way to my door. I had become quite popular as a lawyer with the transsexual community, probably because I treated these ladies as valued clients (and they were) and not as freaks (which they weren't).

Most of my transsexual clients took enormous care with their appearance, perhaps because they had the hurdle of masculine features to overcome. Some went as far as having cranio-facial surgery to make their features more feminine, reducing brow ridges and trimming Adam's apples and square jaws.

I recall one of these ladies walking into our reception area wearing red stilettos, a black leather miniskirt and a see-through red lace blouse (the top half of her was 'post-op', though she told me she had not yet saved enough to have the bottom half done). Her name was Dee Vine, or so she said. Dee was narrow hipped and big busted, with legs up to her armpits and expertly made up: so stunning that our male office junior walked straight into a solid wooden door, too busy drooling at her and polishing his glasses to watch where he was going. At the time, he was the only male in an office full of women, and he was teased mercilessly about this incident. He resigned soon after and I still feel guilty about it.

Another of my transsexual clients was an elegant older lady with grey hair swept up in a Katharine Hepburn style, who would not have been out of place at an English garden party. She was a cultured and well-read Alpaca breeder. There is no way she would ever have countenanced earning a living the way Dee did.

Dee made her income from liaisons with selected gentlemen who were unaware of her previous gender. I always wondered how they would not realise her original bits were still there, but never summoned up the courage to ask for the graphic details. She sometimes also worked as a stripper, and she told me that she managed to hide the telltale dangly bits with Elastoplast. Even under the ultraviolet lights the punters could not see what she had tucked back between her legs. I did not envy her removing the Elastoplast.

Dee did have a certain style, however. Witness the circumstances which first brought her to my office: she had been having some difficulty working in the summer heat—given the fairly vigorous nature of her occupation, this was quite understandable. She solved that quite simply. She hired a cab, directed it to a building site close to her home, had the driver wait while she liberated an air conditioner appropriate for her needs, loaded it into the cab's boot and then had the driver take her to her home address, where she managed to unload it and install it. She couldn't work out how the police knew where to find her!

The help Doreen needed (I thought to myself before she opened her mouth) was a complete makeover. Doreen had no dress sense whatever.

'They want to call me Barry'

'Hello, I'm Judith. How can I help you?' I said in my best 'efficient lawyer' voice, still trying to absorb what I was seeing.

Doreen immediately burst into tears, 'They want to call me Barry,' she sobbed, in a curious mixture of falsetto and baritone.

'Who wants to call you Barry?' I asked, thinking that this was hardly a criminal law problem.

'It's the only thing that matters to me. I don't care if I go to gaol. But I want to go to a women's gaol. I have to go to women's gaol. I couldn't go to any other gaol. It's not fair. All I want is to be called Doreen. Why doesn't anyone have any respect for me? I'm not a freak. I've worked all my life for this. I'm not Barry …'

She stopped to draw a shuddering breath, and I interrupted quickly. 'OK, you've come to see me and I'm a criminal lawyer. Have you been charged with some sort of crime?'

'Yes, but that doesn't matter: what really matters is that I'm not being treated as a woman, which I am.'

'Tell me what happened.'

'They won't call me Doreen, they want to call me Barry, I want to go to a women's gaol …' I had learnt from past dealings that if you are 'pre-op' you go to a man's gaol, and if you're 'post-op' you go to a women's gaol. Clearly, going to a male prison is a tad dangerous for the feminine-looking pre-op transsexuals, though looking at Doreen ('call me Dore'), I thought she could look after herself in a bout of fisticuffs.

This conversation went on for about 15 minutes, during the course of which I extracted from her the fact that she had been charged with what is known as 'unlawful wounding' which in this case meant that she was alleged to have knifed somebody in the back. Leaving out her constant complaints about not being called Doreen, this was the essence of her story and the reason for her presence in my office.

Doreen was indeed a transsexual. This is not to be confused with a transvestite (men who enjoy being dressed in women's clothes, but never cease to be men psychologically). She had always known that she was a woman and was simply unfortunate enough to have a man's body. She was also unfortunate enough to grow quite tall and develop a heavy build. As a woman, the word 'plain' would have been complimentary.

Doreen had been prospecting for semiprecious gems in a very rough outback Australian town where men are most definitely men and women are few and far between (and can run very fast). It is so hot that many of the dwellings are constructed underground in order to survive the searing heat. A man in such an environment has to be handy with his fists. The qualities needed to survive as a transsexual in a town like that I could not begin to imagine. I admired Doreen already.

Over the preceding 18 months, Doreen had gathered quite a haul of fairly poor quality small gemstones and had come to the 'big smoke' to make some money. She had acquired some timber chunks carved into the shape of maps of Australia (minus poor old Tasmania, of course), varnished them, and then glued gemstones on to represent each state capital. They were dreadful, and eminently suitable for the tourist market.

Doreen's idea was that she would sell these jarrah masterpieces and make her fortune. She intended to raise the $35,000 required for her longed-for surgery this way. She was at pains to emphasise that the surgery was 'gender reassignment' surgery, and woe betide anyone who suggested it was called a 'sex change' . The term 'gender reassignment' was a careful choice of language to convey the fact that Doreen had always been a woman and was simply changing her external appearance to match the gender she had always been. Calling the surgery 'sex change' would be suggesting that she wasn't a woman before, and this she and other transsexuals strongly rejected, for obvious reasons.

Ripped off

Doreen's sobs had died down by now. She blew her nose loudly and continued. She had been staying in a very cheap dosshouse in Perth, and had met a young man also staying there, who promised to take her maps of Australia and other assorted gemstones and sell them for her quickly—and at a large profit, of about $40,000. The trusting Doreen agreed, handed over her hard-dug assets, and sat back to await her profits.

The young man returned a few days later, reeking of bourbon, and minus all Doreen's stock, with the paltry sum of $1500 to show for it. She was bitterly disappointed, and unimpressed with the young man's explanations. That money was everything to her: her hopes, dreams and future. A fight broke out on the stairs in the lodging house and somehow ('I don't know how, I really don't,' Doreen wailed), the young man ended up with a knife wound to his back.

Doreen had immediately become hysterical, and disappeared. The police found her at the bar next door, weeping into her beer, 'I've killed him. I just know I've killed him.' When they entered the dingy tavern, she smashed her beer glass against the counter and melodramatically tried to slash her wrists. There was lots of blood but not much damage. The first officer on the scene, being a little less enlightened in the 1980s than police are today, shouted to his colleagues, 'It's got AIDS, don't touch it.' Doreen told me that this was a very common reaction when people realised that she was biologically male, and that she found it very offensive and hurtful. I don't blame her, as it shows a fundamental misunderstanding of what transsexuals are about.

In due course Doreen was arrested, took part in a videotaped interview, as is usual, was charged with unlawful wounding, made a brief appearance in court where nothing much happened, and was then released on bail on a promise to come back to court after getting some legal advice.

The idea was that she would decide whether to plead guilty and fling herself on the mercy of the judge, or not guilty and have a trial where twelve jurors would decide whether the prosecution had proven beyond a reasonable doubt that she did the deed and she had no defence.

Given the fact that there were plenty of witnesses saying that the young man did not have a stab wound before the fight with Doreen, had one immediately afterwards and there was no-one else involved in the fight, I already had my doubts about her chances. I was also a bit worried about how jurors would react to Doreen's unusual appearance.

I watched the videotape of the police interview with Doreen. It had been given to me as part of the 'disclosure papers'. In our justice system, it is considered fair and fundamental that an accused person should know just what is being alleged against them. All relevant evidence ought to be, and mostly is, routinely supplied to an accused or his or her lawyer in advance of the trial including any information the prosecution holds which might help the defence. This is called 'disclosure'.

In the interview, Doreen denied strenuously ever stabbing the young man, and said she had no idea how he ended up with a knife wound in his back. Strangely, in the records which contained the witness statements, the police had not reported finding a knife, though if the eyewitnesses were to be believed she clearly had neither the time nor the opportunity to dispose of it.

I got to know Doreen quite well over the ensuing months. She continued to deny vehemently ever having stabbed anyone in her life, although she agreed she had used her fists forcefully and with damaging results on plenty of occasions before, usually with considerable justification. She seemed to be genuine and I couldn't see why she would want to lie to me. I was at a loss to know what to make of what I had been told.

I also got to the bottom of her complaints about being called Barry. Doreen had found herself with nowhere to live after her arrest. The place where the stabbing occurred would not have her back, perhaps understandably, so she approached a local charitable organisation, whose minions insisted on putting her in a men's boarding house and calling her Barry, which evidently was the name her parents had given her on her Birth Certificate. This was her biggest problem and the main reason she came to see me. The business about unlawful wounding was a minor irritant to Doreen, compared with the issue of being treated as a man when she wasn't one.

I did tell her that I didn't know how we were going to win the trial. I told her what her chances were—lousy— and I told her that if she went to trial and was found guilty she would miss out on the gold stars and brownie points (in other words a lighter sentence) the courts give out for pleading guilty early and saving the public the expense and the victim the distress of the trial. Still, there was no way I was going to tell her to plead guilty if she was adamant she had not done the stabbing.

Innocent people have looked guilty before. I thought of Lindy Chamberlain, who was convicted of murdering her infant daughter, and years later was exonerated and awarded over $1 million in compensation. She had argued that a dingo took the infant at a camp site near Ayers Rock (now Uluru). Probably well over half of all Australians believed she was guilty at the time of her original trial. Part of the reason for this was prejudice due to her membership of a minority religious group

We were going to have to deal with the possibility of prejudice in Doreen's upcoming trial too. I had had enough strange reactions when I told friends or colleagues that I had represented transsexuals to convince me that many people were still extraordinarily unenlightened.

Eureka

Then, about a month before the trial, I was looking again at the crime scene photographs taken by the police photographer. The fight had taken place on the stairs in the dosshouse. There was a plastic bag just visible in the corner of one of the photographs of the stairs. I hadn't really focussed on it before. The bag had a split in it.

I asked Doreen, 'Whose bag is that?'

'Mine.'

'What was in it?'

'I was cooking me dinner upstairs and it had all me dinner stuff in it.'

'Like what?' I asked, already having some idea of what I was going to hear.

'Me bread, me margarine, me steak, me fork, me knife.'

He Fell on the Knife

'Your knife? What sort of knife?'
'Me pocket knife.'
'Was it open?'
'Yes, of course.'
'Was it sharp?'
'Well, duh, of course it was.'

I caught my breath. I knew what must have happened. I could see that for the first and probably only time in my career, I was going to run the 'he fell on the knife' defence. At least I wasn't going to have to say, 'He fell on the knife and then jumped up and fell on the knife two or three more times.' There was, thank heavens, only the one stab wound.

We already had a trial. We now had a defence. The game was on!

I knew from long experience that having a defence did not necessarily mean an acquittal. There was much more to be accomplished first and, even after scrupulous preparation, outcomes are sometimes in the laps of the gods.

First I had to get Doreen prepared to give evidence. Aside from me knowing what she was going to say, there was also the question of her dress sense. This was very important to her and also to me: clothes maketh the man or woman in court. It is easy to alienate a jury or a judge by dressing as if for a day at the beach. It shows you don't take the proceedings seriously.

I have often given sartorial advice to clients, suggesting

a drug dealer lose the designer stubble, and the bouncer lay off the steroids before the trial.

Doreen asked, 'Shall I come secretary, or astronaut?'

Having visions of silver lamé with the astronaut look, I suggested she 'come secretary'. Big mistake.

On the day of trial, I realised, too late, what 'secretary' meant to her. Doreen turned up in a blue sequined cocktail dress, with a pair of white shoes which could have been used as boats, a pair of white gloves and a white handbag. The red lipstick wasn't too dreadful, but the 'fascinator' hat with a little veil was not a good look. I suppose at least the blue eye shadow matched the dress.

I gave Doreen a pep talk, reminding her to tell the truth. I then delivered her to the detention area where she was to wait during all the breaks in the trial day, so as not to run into jurors. The days when a person, having been out on bail and waiting for their trial to begin, had to go to prison each night during the trial in case they ran into a juror had ended only recently. At least Doreen would go home (wherever that was) at night.

I knew we were going to have to introduce the subject of transsexuality to the jury, both to explain why she looked as she looked and to explain why she was so upset and angry at the time of the fight. She hadn't been charged with assaulting the 'victim', that is thumping him, which she had undoubtedly done, but with wounding him. Obviously she had to tell the jury in her own words what had happened in order to explain the knife wound. This had to include the fistfight.

Accused people do not have to give evidence in a trial, as the rule is always that the prosecution has to prove beyond a reasonable doubt that the accused did the dastardly deed. Hence, a person can simply say to the prosecution, 'You say I did it: you prove it!' Sometimes, though, they would be crazy not to give evidence, as they are the only ones who can explain or give a version of events different from the prosecution's.

We did some rehearsing of her responses to questions in the dock. For example, how to explain gender reassignment surgery to the jury who may not have come across this before in their everyday lives.

The whole truth

Picture this: a wood-panelled courtroom. The judge, a round-faced man of about 60, with broken capillaries in his cheeks and on his bulbous nose, wearing black, red and purple robes and a big off-white horsehair wig, seated behind a large table raised above the rest of the courtroom, the State Coat of Arms above and behind him. The jury box, with its seats arrayed in two rows of six, along one wall of the courtroom, the judge to the jurors' right, the lawyers just to their left and the dock holding the accused directly across from them. Barristers in their black gowns, black waistcoats and white jabots (a type of cotton bib) wearing smaller horsehair wigs behind two long, red leather-covered tables running almost the complete width of the courtroom.

The jury officer (a motherly woman in black blazer and pinstriped skirt), the judge's associate, sometimes called the clerk of arraigns (a retired 'ex-military' chappie wearing a uniform similar to the jury officer's, only with trousers, not a skirt), and the usher (a weedy little man in a similar uniform whose main job seemed to be running errands, when not doing the crossword and dozing during slow bits of the trial), all in their assigned chairs. Three uniformed police officers in the back of the court, another police officer waiting in the dock to guard the accused, Doreen, when she was brought up from the detention cells as if from a dungeon beneath the court.

The jury pool, about 60 people chosen at random from the electoral roll (minus some occupational groupings, such as lawyers, priests and firemen, who are automatically excluded) waited in the public area of the courtroom to see whether they were to be chosen as jurors in this trial. It was fairly chilly and uncomfortable for all but the lawyers. The air conditioning was turned up high enough to keep the lawyers and judge comfortable in their woollen gowns, bar jackets and wigs. (On very hot days in country courthouses where the air conditioning is not powerful or non-existent, some incredibly liberal judges will sometimes allow lawyers to remove their wigs.)

'Put up the accused,' announced the associate. Enter

Doreen, 'secretary' Doreen, into the witness box. There was a gasp from the potential jurors as she appeared. Their mouths were too far open to speak for a moment, then a buzz of loud whispers started. The associate coughed to quieten the jurors and then asked the required question, 'Barry Smith—is that your name?'

'No, my name is Doreen.' I had already tipped off the judge, via his associate, that we were likely to strike this difficulty in the very first moments of the trial. His Honour, quite enlightened, had agreed that he would not make a big issue about the name, provided I confirmed in writing that the person on trial really was the person who was meant to be on trial. I had done this. So the first problem was smoothly overcome.

The jury selection began. Unlike the American crime shows we are inundated with, in Australia there is no questioning of potential jurors to find out their beliefs and foibles. All a Western Australian defence barrister in those days was allowed to know was their name, address and occupation. These days lawyers don't even get a name, just a number. The prosecution used to be told, in addition, whether or not they have a criminal record.

At the time of Doreen's trial, defence barristers were only permitted to challenge (or arbitrarily remove) five jurors in the selection process. Our reasons were usually as simple as 'I don't like the look of him', or perhaps if your client had been charged with robbing a bank, you might challenge a bank manager's suitability.

The names were drawn from a box, a bit like drawing the winning raffle number. Some looked thrilled, some unimpressed. I challenged the first five men. My theory was that women would be more sympathetic to Doreen. As it turned out, what happened during the trial would have tested anyone's sympathy.

The 12 jurors sat in the jury box, notebooks and pens in front of them, ready to pay attention and do justice as they saw it. I thought I'd done pretty well by getting a majority of women in the jury.

Fast forward to day three of the trial: the poor little victim had told his story and been cross-examined up hill and down dale by me in an attempt to paint Doreen as the true victim. The police had described in detail what happened when they arrived at the scene.

Then, enter Doreen, 'secretary' Doreen again (thank heavens, she had not changed to 'astronaut' Doreen overnight), into the witness box. She was wearing another fetching outfit. This time, a yellow crimplene number, a trouser suit with yet another pair of large, white shoes. She wore a corsage for the occasion. She was a vision.

We went through her evidence chronologically. She told the jury what happened. We got to the really hard bit, the bit we had rehearsed many times over, which went a little bit like this: 'Please tell the members of the jury why you were so upset with this man.'

'He took me money.'

'What was the money for?'

'It was for me operation.' A tear trickled down Doreen's cheek. She blew her nose into a large white handkerchief, very loudly. So far, so good. All was going according to plan. I could see the jurors leaning forward, looking sympathetic.

The next bit had been rehearsed and rehearsed. 'What was your operation for? Was it to make you look more feminine?' Here we go. We were about to explain 'gender reassignment' to this overwhelmingly middle class conservative jury.

'No.' This was not going according to plan: this was not the answer we had rehearsed. She paused. The courtroom seemed to shrink. All eyes were on Doreen. We waited for an answer.

Doreen took a deep breath and blurted out, 'No, it was just to cut me dick and the rest off—nothin' would make me look feminine!'

The seconds following that comment seemed interminable. I felt sick. The judge glared at me. I looked for somewhere to hide. I could feel rather than see the jury sitting there with their jaws on their laps. Doreen was looking around as if to say, 'What have I said?' I was trying to find a way to communicate the thought, 'This wasn't MY idea, your Honour, honestly.' I thought, fleetingly, of the newly convicted man who, when asked if he had anything to say before he was sentenced, could only reply, 'Beam me up, Scotty!' Where's the teleporter when you really need one?

As soon as I could breathe again, I went on to the next question and tried to pretend nothing had happened. I finished questioning Doreen quickly, and then sat down.

At the end of the trial, as we awaited the verdict, I sat in the deserted courtroom and reflected.

The whole experience had been surreal. There was Doreen in her secretary clothes, doing nothing worse than being completely honest, and yet I was worried about it. And who was in drag anyway? I was wearing black robes left over from past centuries, supposedly still in mourning for some king or queen or other, and a horsehair wig! The judge in his multicoloured splendour looked a bit like a liquorice allsort, albeit a very important liquorice allsort. I think we looked far stranger than Doreen.

We have a verdict

The buzzer from the jury room sounded, startling me. The jury had been deliberating for less than half an hour. The jury officer looked at me, stunned: 'We have a verdict.'

Lawyers were hurriedly tracked down by phone, wigs were replaced, till all were present and accounted for, ready to hear the verdict.

Doreen was brought up from the holding cells. She stood in the dock flanked by two guards, and faced the jury, big white handkerchief at the ready.

I felt even sicker. I should have rehearsed her more. I should have insisted on looking at what she was planning

He Fell on the Knife

to wear. I should have told her not to use four-letter words. I should have, I should have, I should have … the list went on.

'How say you, members of the jury? Is the accused guilty or not guilty?' asked the associate, who had transmogrified into the clerk of arraigns, in the archaic language of the criminal court.

The grandmotherly forewoman consulted the pad she was holding, drew herself up to her full 150 centimetres and replied, 'We find the accused not guilty.'

'Is that the verdict of you all?'

'Yes,' replied the forewoman, smiling at Doreen, 'and we wish her all the best.'

I would like to say that the courtroom erupted in cheers, but the truth is that Doreen had no friends in the public gallery to support her. She was just a 'girl' from out of town, trying to become what she always knew she was. We looked at each other, and she mouthed the words 'Thank you.'

After the court was adjourned, I went over to Doreen and she enveloped me in an enormous hug. I felt like crying. Though all my cases were important to me, for some reason, this case had mattered more than most.

I suspect Doreen was acquitted because the jury thought that no-one could have come out with the answers she did without being completely honest. But I will never know for sure.

I saw Doreen some years later at a street market stall,

still selling her semiprecious stones. She recognised me and I could not help but recognise her: same bad dress sense, and the same bad colour scheme.

She insisted on giving me a pendant: a piece of crystal, chipped, badly glued onto a ring through which was threaded a nylon cord burnt at each end to prevent fraying, and then knotted. Her latest handcrafted souvenir, made with love.

Doreen may recognise herself in this story, and if she does, I hope she realises that I have spoken of her with affection. Many years later, I still keep the pendant pinned to my office noticeboard, along with cards and pictures which bear with them memories of special and brave people who have had an impact on me. Whenever I think my job or life is hard, I think of Doreen.

Nutters and Nasties

The practice of criminal law attracts some very strange people, and by this I do not necessarily mean the lawyers, though they are plenty strange enough. There is a certain breed of client which I soon learnt to spot from a distance of approximately 200 metres. They have been dubbed 'querulous paranoiacs' by an eminent lawyer of my acquaintance. I will call them 'problem clients'.

These people have been known to type letters over 12 pages long in a very small font, with EXCESSIVE USE OF CAPITALS and exclamation marks!!!!! As well as asterisks**** to EMPHASISE every SECOND word, they also use highlighters in every colour known to humanity, and often present you with a poor photocopy of a letter outlining the long and sorry history of their case.

In the old days, I suspect problem clients had the market in geriatric typewriters cornered. If the letter was not presented as a poor photocopy, it was presented as a letter typed in the old-fashioned way on both sides of the flimsiest airmail paper with the paper insides of the 'e' and 'o' often missing, punched out by the force of the keystrokes. Coffee mug rings were the look *du jour*. There was often reference made to legal principles and cases, and legalese used with no understanding at all of the law. Much library, and nowadays internet, searching clearly went on for what looked like the right terminology.

There would inevitably be a conspiracy among members of officialdom including the local council, the neighbours, and at least five previous lawyers, all of whom were to be sued, as a MATER * OF * PRINCIPEL!!!. (They could not spell either). The Ombudsman would be in on the plot, too, if he had not responded to the flood of mail with immediate action. Extra copies of their letters would be sent to Members of Parliament, the Queen Mother, the Prime Minister and the Archbishop of Canterbury, as well as being kept in a bank vault in case of foul play. They would ask for the lawyer's home telephone number and home address in case they needed to telephone at 3am with a new defendant to add to the list, or visit with an additional mountain of urgent documents. The actual problem was usually something incredibly serious like the question of who should pay for repairs to a dividing fence, or one of Australia's spy agencies bugging the client's pumpkin patch.

One client alleged that ASIO was operating from outer space and tapping into the wires supporting his very large cannabis plants and listening in to his conversations. He complained to the local police about ASIO's efforts and was puzzled when he was charged with cultivating cannabis. Another, whose name was 'Snowball', was charged by the police with threatening to kill. In the early hours of the morning he had telephoned a young constable, saying that he was going to send cancer-causing chemicals down the telephone line if that officer did not take his complaints seriously. Frankly, I thought charging him with a criminal offence was probably pandering to his paranoia and would not achieve very much at all.

These people have, as far as I can tell, failed to notice the advent of computers for word processing purposes, would not know a spell-checker if it bit them on the backside, and yet have passionately embraced email with its capacity to copy and scatter allegations to the four corners of the earth. Here is an actual example of one of these missives (with some details changed to protect the guilty).

Subject: Re: YOUR LIES!!!!!

you're WRONG WRONG WRONG FRENCH.... you played right into my hands I am going to take it allto the cleaners.You think you've got all your own wayand you have the whole legal systemat your beck and callwhen you got another think coming ... you have committedfraud andany number ofother CRIMINAL acts,,, I have proofthat I will not rest till JUSTICE!!!!! is done

I am sending a fax to your boss, the Premier,the chief justice, all you are snivelling little mates to let them know about your *crimes*! to name a few usury, perjury, running bawdy house, perverting justice, itismydutyasacitizenofthisgreatcountrytoshowhimand all of them what you are up to and the**LIES** you are telling ... did you say I am a criminal, well you are the criminal you have committed so many unspeakable crimesand it is time the **WORLD KNEW!!!!** you have breached 27 separate Acts of Parliament of this countryand also 217 laws of the US of A.

I will have you ... GiNY

We had a special technique for dealing with problem clients. The first step was to ask for a substantial deposit, because inevitably they wanted the lawyer to put in hundreds of hours of time, urgently, and equally inevitably could not grasp the concept of payment for services rendered. The second and crucial step was to compose a CYA letter and ask the client to sign it. 'CYA' stood for 'Cover Your Bottom'. It was along these lines:

'I, Mr Bloggs, acknowledge that my lawyer has told me that the action I want to take (1) is certain to fail (2) is going to cost me more money than I have (3) will not achieve anything at all and (4) will ensure that I am committed to a secure unit of a psychiatric institution sooner than would otherwise occur. Despite all this advice I am instructing my lawyer to take this action.'

Such a letter never seemed to stop the client adding us to the long list of conspirators when the desired result did not eventuate, but it certainly made us feel better. Luckily, no one else (like the Legal Practicioners Complaints Committee) took much notice of them either.

Ex-tortion

My ex-husband shared some of the characteristics of problem clients. After I began practising as a lawyer, he had evidently noticed a story about one of my cases in his local newspaper. Shortly after, I received a letter from him asking me to pay him $750,000 in equal monthly instalments over the next 18 months, failing which he was going to write to any number of interested parties about my supposed misdeeds, frauds, crimes, promiscuity and general moral bankruptcy. I suppose in today's terms that would equate to more like $2 million. However much it was, I didn't have it, and was not going to pay it. I wrote back and said so very clearly. Two or three months went past. All was quiet, and I thought (OK, I hoped) that he may have been run over by a bus or was at the very least terminally ill, bedridden and dying a slow and painful death, preferably with suppurating sores.

No such luck: a copy of a letter arrived and I immediately recognised his handwriting. This letter had been sent to the State police, the Federal police, the Chief Justice of Western Australia, the State Director of Public Prosecutions, the Commonwealth Director of Public Prosecutions, and three or four other agencies. It was one way of becoming known to these various departments, but certainly not the way I had in mind to progress my career. Among other dreadful misdeeds, my ex-husband alleged that I had committed fraud by conspiring with the bank manager (with whom, he firmly believed, I had had a sexual relationship) to forge his signature on a bridging finance application for a house we had purchased together.

I was angry, embarrassed and ready to defend my honour. Thankfully by this stage I knew a little bit about law and knew that the whole point of fraud is that the perpetrator gets some sort of benefit by some sort of trickery or deceit. I had some difficulty seeing what the benefit was meant to be, when the bridging finance had been paid off by the sale of a property owned solely by me (I hasten to add that I had not forged his signature). I took the trouble to ring the bank manager and tell him that he and I had been having a sexual relationship. It was news to him.

Police have to take any complaint of criminal conduct seriously, and I suspect that when a lawyer is alleged to have done something naughty they take even more care to be scrupulous in their investigation and to be seen to be scrupulous. Hence I had to be interviewed by the State police. The police, who seem to always travel in pairs, came to my office by appointment rather than turning up when I was with a client, for which I was grateful. I totally ignored my usual advice to my own criminal law clients, which was, 'Say nothing at all.' The interview wasn't much fun. The whole situation was extremely uncomfortable. I think my ex-husband was banking on me being so embarrassed or frightened that I would pay up to keep him quiet. He was wrong. In due course, once I had shown them the documents about paying out the loan, the police pronounced themselves quite happy that I had not committed any criminal offence.

I still see one of these officers from time to time in my role teaching police the law of evidence, and I am now able to see the funny side and have a chuckle with him about it. At the time, though, when I was just starting my legal career, I was not amused. Although I don't think anyone took what my ex had said seriously, it still gave me an embarrassing public profile. He had managed to write to a large number of people, all working for or in charge of agencies I dealt with on a daily basis. If nothing else, he was thorough.

Luckily for me, my ex-husband had made the same mistake most of these obsessed people make, namely coming up with allegations so ridiculous that no-one takes them seriously. The best one of all was the suggestion that I had broken into the Family Court building in the dead of night and stolen documents from the files. That was a doozy! I can just see me in my black cat burglar suit shinning up the drainpipe and climbing through the bathroom window in the Family Court. Just my style.

The State police, to the best of my knowledge, still wish to speak to my ex-husband about his unsuccessful extortion attempt should he ever set foot in Western Australia.

Peace on earth, goodwill to men

Although criminal law tends to attract eccentric or just plain mad people, be they lawyers or clients (or, dare I say, judges), there are not many in any of these categories who are thoroughly nasty or evil. Even my killers could be thoughtful.

It was Christmas Eve, perhaps 15 years ago. Close to midnight, my telephone rang. I must have been the only lawyer in town answering calls. It was Mrs Barker, ringing because her son had been arrested for wilful murder. Between wrenching sobs, the tale unfolded.

Christmas for many people is a time of joy and thanksgiving. For others, it is the time of misery or stress. I would not be surprised if statistics proved that the murder rate did actually peak at such times. For Denny (the son in question), it was a time of misery. His wife had left him that day, and taken their two children with her. She had moved in with someone Denny knew was an amphetamine dealer.

Denny was left at home in an empty house with the children's Christmas presents still under the tree. He sat in the strangely silent house and fretted. His wife had been a drug user and he was worried that she had taken up the habit again.

He was hurting, deserted and fearing for his children. He drove to the nearby street where his family was now living, walked towards the block of flats, and stared up at the lighted window. He shed tears, whether of rage or pain he could not say.

Denny conceived a plan. He would confront this wife-stealing, child-stealing drug dealer, have it out with him, then take his family back home where they belonged, safe and happy for Christmas together. There was one problem: Denny had quite a slight build and was not in the best of health. The drug dealer's nickname was 'Tiny' because he wasn't.

Denny picked his way across the waste ground towards the flats and squeezed through the fence. At that point a partial solution to the imbalance in size dawned on him. He turned back to the fence, grabbed a loose paling and worked it away from the fence.

The fence paling had long, rusty, lethal-looking nails sticking out of it. Denny grabbed a rock and bashed the nails in. He didn't want to kill anyone, he just wanted to teach Tiny a lesson. He marched up to the flat and stormed through the door, hoping to catch Tiny by surprise.

Tiny was sitting watching television. As Denny swung the paling, Tiny simply reached up, grabbed it and disarmed Denny. The tables were turned. Tiny was bashing Denny with the paling. Denny, on his knees, reached into his hip pocket, withdrew his penknife and stabbed Tiny. It was a little penknife: talk about a lucky (or unlucky, depending on how you look at it) stab. Tiny dropped to the floor with a knife wound to the heart, and died very quickly and messily.

Denny was, quite understandably, charged with wilful murder. Wilful murder simply means you meant to kill the victim, as opposed to murder, where you 'merely' want to hurt them badly and and end up killing them in the process, or manslaughter, where you don't even want to hurt them badly but still end up killing.

At the trial, Denny's immense thoughtfulness in bashing in the rusty nails so they would not hurt Tiny too badly saved the day for him. The jury convicted him of manslaughter, convinced that there was no way he had meant to kill Tiny (or maybe they were just being merciful to Denny because they could understand how he must have felt that Christmas Eve bereft of wife and children).

Denny went to gaol for a couple of years and is now out, working hard, making a good living and lucky in love again, with a brand new 'missus'.

I have represented lots of alleged or actual murderers over the years. When I look at the domestic situation in which murders happen, I often see a man who is otherwise a good parent, a contributing member of the community, often without so much as a traffic ticket in his life. But behind this law-abiding unexceptional public presentation lie terrible problems with the marriage or relationship.

The man, being a typical Australian male, doesn't seek help or counselling from friends or professionals. He has a 'she'll be right, mate' attitude. And then, for complex and sometimes unfathomable reasons, he kills his wife. He is convicted and locked up in gaol for many years with career criminals with whom he has nothing in common, and who are hardly a good, rehabilitative influence on him. It is all, so very often, avoidable.

Happy families are tragically destroyed when large amounts of alcohol, a domestic argument and a weapon within easy reach are combined. There is always a sharp weapon easily to hand in a domestic kitchen. (When I look at the photographs of the victim in such cases, I often think that it could so easily have been me.)

One of my murderers (yes, I do think of them as 'my' murderers, which is possibly a bit odd) was not leaving anything to chance. He turned up at his estranged wife's house with handcuffs, rope, sleeping pills, a set of butchers' knives borrowed specially for the occasion, and some cannabis. I would have had a hard time arguing that the killing was not premeditated, so I didn't even try. The fact that he had left a series of audiotapes discussing his misery and spelling out just how and why he planned to kill her was also not a good start for a successful defence.

Another client who killed his wife was a leader of the local Samoan community. He remained respected by many despite his dreadful act. Following the trial I was invited by the community to their annual Independence Day celebrations. This involved eating an enormous amount of food seemingly all cooked in coconut cream, then wearing a lei, and having to dance or risk causing offence. I'm not very good at dancing at the best of times, and South Pacific style dancing was not really my thing. I did some sort of version of a hula, and have never felt more silly in my life, but I was honoured to have been asked.

Mad, not bad

I have always had a soft spot for my truly insane clients. Schizophrenia is an illness that can often be controlled by medication, but sometimes those who have the illness will feel so well they stop their medication. Sometimes the illness sneaks up on them and the person does not realise they becoming ill again. When the illness is under control, my schizophrenic clients can be delightful people: many have a sense of humour and are good natured, polite and grateful for some help. Some are good cooks, some are studying for high school or academic qualifications, some continue their romantic relationships with partners while in the locked wards at the hospital. On many occasions they have killed someone during an acute phase of their illness, often someone who loved and cared for them. The way they killed may have been horrific. And yet they are worthy of respect, and I can honestly say that I like them. They have an illness. That illness may have had tragic consequences, but it does not stop them being good people.

They are usually charged with wilful murder and mostly acquitted on the basis of insanity. If they are acquitted, they are not left to roam around the streets. They go to a secure psychiatry facility and are not released till their psychiatrists certify they are sane.

Sometimes I have to shake my head at the things that happen to such clients. I recall one young man who was struggling with voices he was hearing. The voices were ordering him to do things (so-called command hallucinations). On his wanderings he encountered two missionaries, or door-to-door religious salesmen, and told them he could hear a voice telling him to do things. The men of God cheerfully assured him that he was hearing the voice of God and that he ought to obey, as it was the Holy Spirit speaking to him. This reassured my client no end: clearly he was not going mad after all. So he took their advice and obeyed the 'voice of God', which just happened to be telling him to kill someone. I wonder if the two missionaries ever knew what harm their advice had done.

The families of these people may well be struggling to absorb what their son or brother or father has done (such clients have all been male in my experience). To their credit, they usually rally around the accused and do their best to support him up to his trial and afterwards, in hospital, then out on day, weekend or extended leave. When I deal with or think of these families, I feel enormous compassion and admiration.

Holding my fourth baby, Anni, in Canberra, 1983. I was on welfare, the year before I started Law School.

The travel addict—in the most over-the-top restaurant in Prague, 2005.

The children, late 1983.

My three beautiful daughters: Anni, Maud & Linda at Maud's wedding, 2007.

Fordhams, my own law firm, opens in the main street of Perth, 1990.

On the front deck of our house in Perth, 2005—a big change from the days of poverty!

The workaholic on holiday, 2007.

Associate Professor at Murdoch University, 2006. Courtesy Brian Richards.

Speaking to thousands of primary school young leaders, 2007.

Transport for the flying lawyer—a light plane in the Kimberley.

A client's pride and joy (the jet, not me).

The opening of a new course for police detectives, 2007—I love a man in uniform ...

Director of Public Prosecutions for Western Australia, Robert Cock, enjoys a drink.

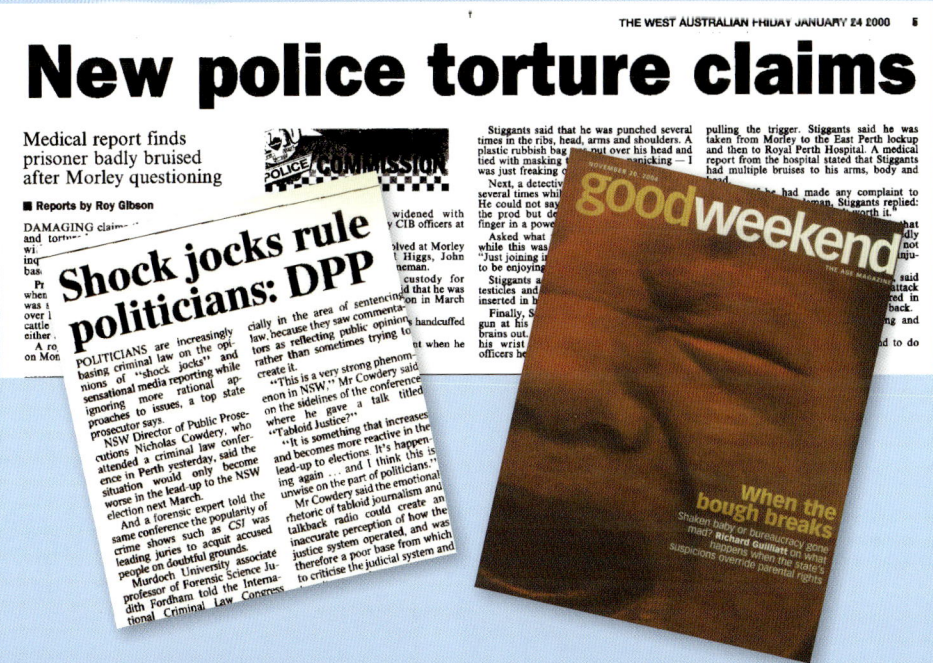

Some of the many articles that are written about my cases and the work which I am involved in.

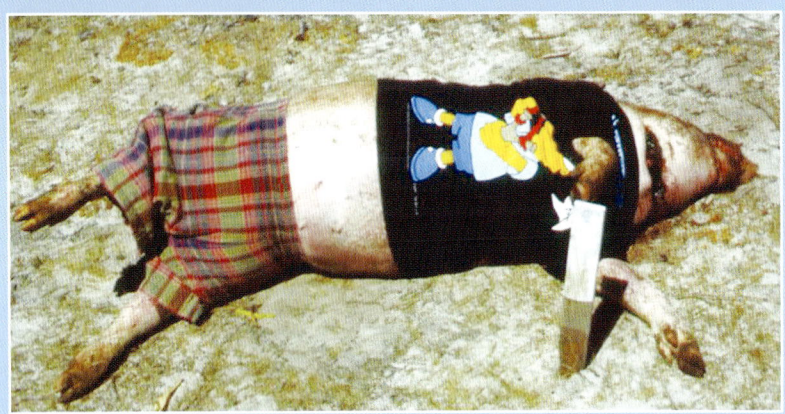

The joys of forensic science: dressing up a dead pig to discover more about maggots and decomposition of human flesh. Courtesy Ian Dadour.

One of my 'different' clients.

Judging Judy

Desmond had a long pink nose and bore more than a passing resemblance to a bandicoot. He was a gentleman of about 60 years of age, a weedy little chap, who wore one of those slightly too luxuriant hairpieces in slightly the wrong colour.

Desmond enjoyed his social life and would quite often bring a young man home for 'fun times', as they say in the personal ads. He had run a series of small businesses over his entire working life, and sometimes sailed a little close to the wind in terms of legality. He didn't like the taxman very much and often gave discounts for cash payment. He was also known as someone to whom one could bring articles of questionable origin, such as video cassette recorders, televisions and mobile phones, and expect a modest sum of cash in return with no questions asked.

Desmond was heading towards retirement age. He had amassed quite a sum of money, all of it the folding variety. Rather predictably, he kept it under his mattress and was understandably upset when one of his boyfriends stole the lot.

Rather than go to the police, he decided to get it back himself. Presumably this had something to do with the source of the money: some of it may have come from the sale of mind-altering substances. It may also have had to do with his failure to pay tax on it. Unfortunately, rather than politely asking for the money back, he took several friends, a baseball bat and an axe. The posse rammed down the door of the wrong house first, and although they did no damage, apologising as they backed sheepishly out, the ungrateful occupants called the police. By the time Desmond and his helpers arrived at the correct house, the police were only minutes behind them. They were caught in the act, inside the house.

I tried to persuade Desmond to plead guilty, but his reasoning was that it was his money, and there was nothing wrong with trying to get it back. Nor was there anything wrong with trying to get it back armed and in a group, as the thief was younger and fitter than him. So, against my advice, Desmond had his day in court.

The trial is not worth talking about. I'm not sure why we even had a trial. He confidently backed up everything the police said about him. At one point during the trial I was doing my bit to suggest to a police officer that he could not be believed in his account of what happened when the police raided my client's house, and that as he was alone at the time there was no-one to corroborate him. He announced confidently from the witness box that my client was present at the raid and would corroborate him. Sure enough, he did.

Inevitably, Desmond was convicted. As the jury had come back fairly late on Friday evening with their verdict, the judge decided not to sentence him then and there, but early the following week instead. Despite the fact that Desmond had been out on bail awaiting for his trial, the judge remanded him in custody: that is, he had to wait in gaol to be sentenced. A remand in custody does not always mean that the client is going to go to gaol in the end. In those days, judges would often send convicted people to gaol for a matter of weeks before they were sentenced to give them a taste of what would happen to them if they did not remain on the straight and narrow after being sentenced to, say, probation. (This doesn't happen any more. It has been seen to do more harm than good, particularly with younger criminals, who are very vulnerable physically.)

Better to be stuck in a lift

The next Tuesday was the appointed day for Desmond's sentencing. I arrived at court fairly early and stood waiting (and waiting) for the lift. It was a little cold in the cavernous beige upon beige lift lobby. I shivered and moved half a step away from the man waiting next to me. I knew I was perfectly safe, but his constant muttered cursing directed to a man who wasn't there was giving me the creeps. After about a thousand years the lift arrived.

The man who was next to me, his friend who wasn't there, and a dozen other people crammed into the lift, which creaked and bounced under our combined weight. A strong smell of body odour and last night's alcohol followed us in. I thought I could identify notes of beer (brand unknown), cask wine and a strong hint of Jack Daniels.

As the lift stopped at the various floors, people left

and entered: court clerks with arms full of files, blue-uniformed police weighed down by their gun belts (for the younger ones) and beer guts (for some of the older ones), skinny young mothers with several barefoot children each, lawyers exchanging morning pleasantries: the usual ebb and flow.

Jack, a defence lawyer and good friend, swept into the lift in his court robes, minus the wig. It is considered rather uncool to wear the wig outside the courtroom in Western Australia, although our eastern states counterparts seem to be happy to wear the full regalia walking down city streets. 'Morning, Judith. You must have something serious on: you've got some law books in your arms. You've got a really bad case if you have to turn to the law!'

I smiled, and at that moment the lift shuddered to a stop, between floors, and the doors creaked and strained attempting to open. 'That's God's way of punishing me for being early to court,' I remarked wryly. Several people chuckled nervously. The lift ground, crunched and lurched into motion again. In retrospect, given what happened later that morning, I would have been better off trapped in the lift, regardless of the foetid atmosphere.

Released, I walked briskly down to the custody area and stood in front of the camera waiting to be recognised and buzzed in. Years earlier, the police in the custody area would assume that I was a prisoner's girlfriend and refuse to let me in, but by this stage they were much better trained. 'How is Ms Fordham today? Left anything behind lately?' said the speaker on the wall to my right. This little dig was aimed at the fact that I had lately specialised in leaving my $700 wig behind in various courtrooms. Strangely, no-one ever tried to steal it. It was an Ede and Ravenscroft (Regalia Makers to the Queen) made-to-measure effort which I had originally thought made me look like a competent lawyer. Lately, however, it had become more of a nuisance, having to be carted around everywhere along with the rest of the archaic gear we lawyers have to wear.

Signed in, I took my place at the row of carrels (stalls). The room was rectangular, divided lengthwise by a glass screen. On one side of the glass the lawyers sat; on the other side were their clients. Communication took place with a telephone handset, and any documents which had to be shown to the client had to be slapped up against the glass screen. As with most of the building, this room was airless and smelt dusty.

'I'm the real victim here, miss'

Desmond scurried in. He actually looked a lot better without his hairpiece, which had not been allowed to come to prison with him, presumably for fear that he might pull it to pieces and knit himself a getaway car. He picked up the phone and wheezed, 'D'ya think he'll make me stay in gaol, Miss? I'm the real victim here, Miss.'

'Desmond, I think he will probably lock you up, because

if somebody steals your money you are supposed to call the police. You're not supposed to go round with five of your friends and some serious weapons, break some doors down and beat up your suspects.'

'But if I called the police, they would ask me where the money came from, Miss.'

'Yes Desmond, that's the price you pay for having money you can't explain away and that you haven't told the taxman about. We'll just have to go into court and see how the judge treats you.'

There was some small prospect that Desmond would not go to gaol, but I was not hopeful, and certainly was not about to give him any false hope. The judge was a very pleasant person, who was invariably as merciful as he could be within the bounds of his role. I had always got on well with him. We will call him Judge Mellow (because he usually was) for the purposes of this story. He may recognise himself, but I do not think anyone else will, which is good.

By the end of the morning, everything which could have been said for Desmond had been said by me. Everything which could have been said against him had been said by the prosecution. The judge wanted to think about what he was going to do with Desmond, and to reread the various reports, references and victim impact statements, so he adjourned for an hour.

When court reconvened, the only thing left was for the judge to pronounce his sentence. As always happens, the judge started by saying how he viewed the circumstances of the offence, and how these related to the sentence he was about to give. I don't know whether the judge was having an off day, or whether I was. In retrospect, I think it was both of us.

As he read out what he had made of the facts, I realised that he had got a couple of things wrong. I didn't want him to sentence Desmond on a version of events that looked worse than it really was, and it was already pretty bad. So I interrupted the judge, which is generally considered a big no-no. The first time I interrupted him he took it quite well, particularly as he had made a genuine mistake. The second time I interrupted him I have to say in all fairness it was a fairly minor point and I probably should have kept my mouth shut. The judge made it clear that he wasn't impressed. The third time I interrupted him I was wrong and the judge had got it right.

It was at that point the steam started coming out of the judge's ears. He slammed his pen down, got up and stormed out of court. After a time he came back, fixed me with a steely glare and announced, 'I am adjourning now and will provide my sentencing remarks in writing. That way Ms Fordham will not get any further opportunity to interrupt me. And, I am telling you now,' he roared, turning to my client, 'you are going to gaol!'

Oh dear. Obviously I had gone far too far, and even Judge Mellow had been pushed beyond all endurance. What was worse, my client now thought it was entirely my fault that he was going to gaol. After I had got over my shock at what had happened, and been to see the client in an unsuccessful attempt to pacify him, I stood in the corridors of the court building. People were walking busily past and around me, but I was oblivious to them all. I was really upset, both at what Desmond thought I had done to him (although I did not believe for a minute that the judge would let my behaviour affect the sentence, it didn't look that way to Desmond), and at what I perceived at the time as the unfairness of it all. I worked myself up into a lather of indignation. I went into a couple of courtrooms at random and sat in the public gallery, simmering, trying to think of what to do.

I telephoned the prosecutor. 'I'm going to go and see the judge about this,' I announced. This was correct etiquette, as my client had not yet been sentenced. It is considered extremely poor form to have private communications with the judge about a case before it is concluded, for obvious reasons. I told the prosecutor that I wanted to explain my reasons for interrupting the judge and generally stick up for myself. The prosecutor, quite wisely, told me I was more than welcome to go and see the judge but to leave him out of it.

What career?

I phoned the judge's associate. An associate is the judge's right-hand man or woman, who sits below and in front of them in court, and acts as their judicial assistant in court and often personal assistant out of court. The associate was a very pleasant young man who asked me to come up there and then. Up I went to the rarefied atmosphere of the upper floors of the building. The associate led me to the door of the judge's chambers (his office) and ushered me in. I thought the associate would come in too, but he did not.

I entered the enormous, plushly carpeted office, which boasted a significant library, a conference table, a sitting area with lounge chairs and coffee table and the usual large desk and executive chair. I was so nervous that it took me a moment to actually spot the judge. He got up from his chair and walked towards me, smiling kindly. I was nonplussed: the last time I had seen him he was roaring at me.

I opened my mouth, ready to say something like, 'I did what I thought was right in court. We are always told to be brave and to fight for our clients. I am sorry if I offended you, but I would do it all again in an instant if I had to.'

Well, that is what I was supposed to say.

It is said that when men get angry, or frustrated or upset, many of them deal with it by being assertive or aggressive. It is also said that when women get angry, or frustrated or upset, many of them cry. Both comments are gross generalisations, to which many members of each gender fail to conform. Unfortunately, I managed to conform comprehensively.

I immediately burst into tears. I was still furious at

the judge, but I was now humiliated as well. So much for being the big tough lawyer. 'I wasn't supposed to do this,' I hiccuped, pointing at my tear-filled eyes. 'I was going to tell you that I did what I had to do in court and that I would do it again and that we are supposed to be fearless for our client's sake and that ... and that ... ' The judge passed me some tissues. He smiled kindly at me again. I felt worse.

'You do seem to have more than your fair share of difficult cases, don't you?' he commented. 'Never mind, perhaps we both went off half-cocked.' I knew this was as close to an apology as I would ever get from a judge, so I agreed that I had lots of difficult cases, sniffled a few times and left as quickly as I decently could.

As I walked away from the court building, I reflected that my career was now down the toilet. Not only had I managed to offend one of the nicest judges in the business, get a client locked up thinking it was all my fault (doing no good at all for the word-of-mouth referrals in the prison system), but I had also been UNPROFESSIONAL and, what is worse, a GIRL! That was it, career over, do not pass 'go'.

Over the ensuing few days, I considered the relative merits of careers in gold prospecting, beachcombing or refuse collection. The following Saturday night I went to a criminal lawyers' social function. Who should I spot, as soon as I walked in, but the very same judge? I looked desperately for somewhere to hide: flower pot, toilet, under the table were all looking good, but he had already seen me. He strode over. I braced myself. 'Ah, Judith, how delightful to see you,' and with that he gave me a peck on the cheek. I realised then that he wasn't mad at me: he probably actually liked me, and what's more my secret was safe with him. It is I who am blabbing, now that I think my reputation can probably stand it.

Now, many years later, I can see the (sort of) funny side. I am sometimes asked for advice by lawyers who have done something silly in or out of court and they are fearful that their careers are over or their humiliation will carry on for years. I make a point of telling them this story. They feel better, immediately.

The case of the impossible rapist

I don't know whether this same judge was cursed with me, or I with him, but we shared many weird trials. The case of the impossible rapist was a good example.

It is not easy in some cases of alleged sexual assault to form an objective view about who is telling the truth. There is rarely any independent evidence of sexual intercourse without consent. There may well be evidence of sexual intercourse but the whole point of aggravated sexual assault or rape is that it is done without consent. Even in unequivocal cases where there are witnesses, or the accused pleads guilty, there are rarely independent corroborative signs of the crime, such as injuries. A woman can be raped and show no physical harm whatever. In this case, the absence of physical signs did not support the prosecution, but nor did it really help the defence.

My client was charged with sexually assaulting a lady in the car park of a busy shopping centre late at night. It was always going to be a difficult case to prosecute as there were no witnesses and no forensic evidence. The lady concerned had complained to police approximately a month after the event had allegedly occurred. This meant that any evidence of semen from my client or bruising from the struggle which she had alleged had taken place was not going to be there. The evidence wasn't going to be there if the rape had happened and it wasn't going to be there if it hadn't. The delay didn't help anyone.

In her evidence the woman concerned said that the reason she had not said anything about the rape earlier was that she had not wanted her boyfriend to be worried about why she had come home very, very late. However, she and her boyfriend fought about where she had been and just what she had been up to. In the end, she told him that she had been raped. He immediately picked up the telephone and called the police. When they arrived, this is what she told them:

'I was out with my girlfriends at a hens' night. We had been to a restaurant, had quite a few drinks and then had all gone our separate ways. We organised a stripper but he didn't show up. We all made sure the bride was loaded into a cab and sent home safely. I didn't think twice about my own safety. We were just at a shopping centre: the same place that I buy my groceries. It wasn't as if it was a nightclub, a casino, or anywhere I might expect trouble. I must admit I was a little bit nervous at the prospect of walking in the dark through the car park, but one of the waiters kindly offered to walk me to my car.

I remember that I was pretty happy and singing as I walked. It might have been "YMCA" and I might have been doing the actions. He had his arm round me, but only because I was a bit unsteady on my feet. When we got to the car, I opened the driver's side door without too much trouble. I hopped in and when I looked around he was in the passenger seat. We sat and chatted for a while. I thought he was quite a nice person to start with, until he made a move on me. He grabbed round the back of my seat to the lever that flips it down and the next thing I knew he was on top of me. He was really big (about 195 centimetres tall) and even though I'm not small, I couldn't stop him, although I struggled. He raped me. I sat and cried for a long time, then I went home. I told my boyfriend about it later as I was too ashamed to say anything in the first place.'

Call me cynical, or call me experienced, but I started to wonder whether what she had reported was actually possible. She drove a Barina, which was hardly the biggest car in the universe. She was tall, and he was taller. She said he was in the passenger seat, at least to start with. There was no information in the Brief for Prosecution (the copy of all the witness statements and other relevant evidence that has to be shown to the defence before a trial) about what she was wearing at the time of the alleged offence. There was no independent evidence of any force having been used, such as bruising or damage to clothing.

There is no rule that says that someone who is being raped has to struggle. It is eminently sensible not to struggle if that seems like the most appropriate way to behave. But this lady said she did struggle, so as a defence lawyer I was perfectly justified in looking at whether there was anything independent of her word to support what she said.

I know there are plenty of jokes (and real-life experience) suggesting that it is perfectly possible, if one puts one's mind to it, to have intercourse in very confined spaces, such as the back seat of a Volkswagen Beetle. The question in this case was whether it is possible to have intercourse in a Barina when one party doesn't want to and is actively resisting. I have always found it helpful to look at the scene of the crime, but unfortunately the car had since been sold. I went off to a car yard owned by yet another client to look at a Barina of the same make and model. The more I looked, the less I could imagine the deed happening in the manner described by the complainant.

Beep beep

The day of trial arrived. Although I had had a look at the statements in the Brief for Prosecution, I did not know precisely what this alleged victim was going to say when I cross-examined her. Nor did I know whether the jurors knew or had experienced just how small a Barina was. There was one way to solve the second problem. I would procure a Barina and let the jurors have a good look at it.

This sounds very easy, but courts are highly controlled places. I could not just suggest to the jury that they go and have a look at a Barina during the trial. The jury is supposed to all receive the same information and it is supposed to be presented in court so that there is some control about how it is presented. The usual way the jury gets to have a look at a crime scene, be it a public street, a house or a motor vehicle is to have a 'view'. This can involve the whole jury piling into a bus, along with security people and court staff, with the judge and lawyers following behind. Everyone then gets out of their respective vehicles and has a good look at the scene. It is often expensive, and not that easy to arrange, and to do so one has to get the judge's approval. Some judges are not particularly easy to convince, partly because of the sheer fuss and bother involved, not to mention security problems.

In any case, I decided it was going to be easier to bring the Barina to the jury rather than the other way around. I had the cooperation of the car yard owner so I asked him how he would feel about me subpoenaing a car to use as evidence. He was happy with that.

I asked the judge if he would approve this course of action. His immediate reaction was, 'Ms Fordham, this smacks of a cheap theatrical trick!'

The best response I could think of was, 'Your Honour, I'm not in the habit of cheap theatrical tricks.' That was hardly a persuasive argument filled with logic and references to the wisdom of past judges. It was just the best I could do on the spur of the moment. I was filled (again) with righteous indignation, which did not help (again). I seemed to specialise in indignation with this judge but at least I did not cry this time. He refused, ruling that nothing but the original car would do. I saw this judge at a dinner recently, years after this trial, and he confessed he said this to get me off his back, knowing that the original car had been disposed of.

This was a challenge: I was in court all day, so I got a message out to our tame car yard man. He used his contacts in the trade, and that evening, with a metaphorical flourish, produced THE car, the one in which the rape had supposedly happened.

The next morning, trying hard not to look smug, I announced to the judge that I had, as requested, located the exact car.

The judge now confesses that he was 'hoist with his own petard'.

My gall may have saved the day. His Honour decided

that he would allow this unusual course of action. I don't think he realised what a circus it would turn into. In my defence, nor did I.

Once the decision had been made that the jury should have a look at the Barina, we then had to get them to it, or (more sensibly) it to them. The judges' car park was in the basement of the building where the trial was, so that was a convenient place to put the Barina and to bring the jury. At least there was some security for the jury and there was no need to load them onto a bus.

The entire court was transferred to the basement. The twelve jurors, the prosecutor, me, the judge, the judge's associate, the usher, the accused, the guards: everyone else and their respective dogs. Everyone bar the jury stood up the other end of the basement car park trying to act as if this was the sort of thing that happened every day. The jurors popped in and out of the car, laid the seat back, and I swear they experimented to see whether one juror could lie on top of another in either of the front seats (or am I imagining that bit?).

Eventually we all trooped back upstairs to the courtroom and I then informed the judge that I would like to tender the car as an exhibit in the trial. The reason for this relates to a technical legal distinction between a 'view' (just having a look at the scene of the crime), and an 'exhibit' which makes the item part of the evidence. I would like to explain this but the distinction has never made much sense to me, so I can't! One of the problems which didn't strike me or anyone else until after the car had become an exhibit was that it then had to be held onto for 21 days after the trial, pending a possible appeal. The new owner was very understanding, but I was probably not popular with the judge who had to park on the street for 21 days, as his or her car space in the basement had been taken by the Barina.

What a man

Lawyers don't often have magic moments. Mostly, for me at least, trials involve lurching from the brink of disaster to the pit of despair, with occasional hummocks of happiness. This trial was an exception. Aside from the Barina fun and games, the responses to my cross-examination gave me some absolutely marvellous material with which to address the jury. Perhaps his Honour did have a point: there was a healthy element of theatre in this trial.

'Ladies and gentlemen, I represent the accused man in this trial. Normally, I would tell you what his version of the events is, and tell you why you should doubt what the complainant, the young lady, has to say. I am going to do something a little unusual today. I am just going to tell you what she has said in her evidence and then leave it to you to make your minds up. I am not going to exaggerate. I'm just going to give you the sequence of events from her own mouth:

'She and the accused walked to her car. The car

was parked in a brightly lit shopping centre car park. He got into the passenger seat. She got into the driver's seat. The car was a Barina. You have seen the Barina downstairs in the car park earlier today. He is 195 centimetres tall. She is 175 centimetres tall. She was wearing, we have discovered, a pair of jeans with a button fly, a body suit and a pair of knickers. The two of them talk for a while, and somehow (we have not been told how) she ends up in the passenger seat.

He lies on top of her. She is still fully clothed. The seat falls back of its own accord. He holds her down with one arm across her chest. With the other hand he undoes her button fly, undoes the press studs on her body suit, and gets her jeans down sufficiently to be able to have intercourse. Whilst he is doing this, with the other hand (ladies and gentlemen, I do hope you are counting along with me: I make this three hands so far) he puts a condom on. She struggles throughout the entire incident, which she says lasts for 45 minutes. For that entire time, whilst she is struggling and whilst he is using all three of his hands, he manages to maintain his erection. Ladies and gentlemen, what a man.'

By this time most of the jurors were laughing, men and women alike. They remembered her evidence. They knew it didn't make sense. They acquitted my client in a matter of minutes.

I have told this story to people before, and some think it fairly poor taste on my part to be able to laugh at something as serious as an allegation of sexual assault. All I can say to those individuals is that to be a criminal lawyer one has to deal with gruesome things, tragic things, disgusting things, quite regularly. Most criminal lawyers develop the ability to see the funny side of such cases or lose their sanity. Most police develop a similar sense of humour. Some forensic pathologists are even worse. It doesn't mean we don't care. It is a way of coping. We are also aware that not every person who is arrested is guilty, and not every alleged victim is telling the whole truth. I don't think I have ever, before or since, used humour when addressing a jury, but this occasion absolutely called for it. And it worked.

Hello?

I got myself into all sorts of trouble in Magistrates Court (or, as it then was, the Court of Petty Sessions) when mobile phones first came onto the market. Being technologically challenged at the time I was not very good at turning the things off reliably. Over the years I have had several embarrassing experiences when these instruments of the devil have gone off in court. Some magistrates and judges possess and display a sense of humour; others may well possess such a thing, but they leave it in a jar by their bed when they come to work, a bit like a pair of false teeth.

My first miserable experience with a mobile phone involved a ring tone which was not very conducive to my serious lawyer image. It may have been the 'Chicken Dance'. I was in court in the middle of applying for an adjournment. My client had not arrived because she was too scared of her ex-partner, against whom she was applying for a restraining order. I had told her that I was fairly confident of our prospects and asked her to give me a call to check the result. Unfortunately, she was a little eager, and called me when I was actually standing, addressing the magistrate. I fumbled for the 'off' button to no avail. The magistrate must have been having a relatively pleasant morning, because all he did was smile at me and state the obvious, 'I think someone wants to speak to you, Ms Fordham.'

It was a relatively small courtroom, with only about 10,000 people laughing at me. Unfortunately, one of those laughing was a representative of our local newspaper, the *West Australian*. I kept on desperately trying to find the 'off' button. The magistrate very helpfully said, 'Why don't you just find out what they want?' Obedient as I always am in court, I answered the phone. On realising who it was, I muttered, 'I'll call you back.'

She wasn't satisfied. She wanted to know what was going on with her case. 'We're going to go for an adjournment,' I whispered.

'What? I can't hear you.'

'I am going to ask the magistrate for an adjournment,' I said, a little louder. It soon became obvious it was too loud. The magistrate, no doubt enjoying himself at my expense, looked around the courtroom, where the normally quiet atmosphere was punctuated by bursts of snorts and giggles by those lacking any self-control, and pronounced, 'I take it your application is for an adjournment.'

I finally found the 'off' button, and cut the client off mid-sentence. I have no idea what happened after that as I was in a haze of humiliation. I know that I got my adjournment. I know I slunk out of court and thought I would never be able to show my face there again. I must have got back to the office somehow, and pretended to my staff that everything had gone wonderfully well and announced my great success.

What I do recall, with excruciating clarity, is the fact that the next morning's newspaper, on the inside of the front cover (in a gossip column creatively entitled 'Inside Cover'), carried a blow-by-blow account, exaggerated for greater effect, of my little performance. I found going in to work that morning and then going on to court a particularly challenging experience!

Sex and Drugs and Rock 'n' Roll

Sex and Drugs and Rock 'n' Roll

If you want sex and drugs and rock 'n' roll, become a criminal lawyer, not a rock star. We deal with sex and drugs for a living: it's only a hobby for rock stars.

My first Supreme Court trial certainly had plenty of sex in it, some drugs, and I expect rock 'n' roll was playing on the fateful evening. I was asked to act for a member of a motorcycle enthusiasts' organisation who had been charged, along with several of his friends, with a pack rape. A pack rape was at the time also known as an 'onion'. I did't know why—I thought it had something to do with layer upon layer. I have only recently discovered, (from a female police officer, no less), that the real reason is that an onion is a root vegetable. Think about it.

The sensationalist local afternoon 'rag' had its circulation boosted, as each day there was something sleazy, outrageous or downright revolting to report from this trial.

The young lady concerned, the 'complainant', had met these gentlemen at a rather down-market hotel, where the entertainment revolved around rock music, smoking tobacco and other substances, drinking, and 'ladies' taking their clothes off on stage. The music thump thump thumped, and red, yellow and green lights flashed on and off in time to the music. The blue light was reserved for the public toilets, as junkies cannot find veins easily under this kind of light. The conversation, on everyone's account, included the complainant telling anyone who would listen that her breasts were superior to those exhibited on the stage. There was also evidence from independent onlookers that she had allowed at least one of the men to conduct a gynaecological examination under the table during the show.

After a few hours, the entertainment started to pall. The boys were ready to move on. This is where the accounts diverge. She says they asked her to 'come to a party'. They said they asked her to 'come and party'. The distinction is crucial.

The group drove back to the house where several of them lived. The security lights (bikers are very security conscious) came on automatically as they approached, lighting up a dusty front yard with the occasional patch of grass. The deadlock was unbolted and the motley bunch staggered in. The house contained worn furniture, motorcycle parts, beer, Bundy and ashtrays overflowing with butts and roaches.

Much sex was had by all four men and one woman. She says she did not want to, and had tried to distract the men by calling a telephone sex line for them. They said she was a willing participant but that things turned a bit ugly when she knocked over one chap's motorbike, which took pride of place in his bedroom. Not the best way to make friends.

On everyone's account, then, she ended up in the car, and was let out on a main road from which she could hitchhike home to the place she and her boyfriend were living. She arrived home as dawn was breaking: a pitiful sight with torn dress and bedraggled hair, smelling of beer and stale cigarettes. The boyfriend was not impressed. She told him she had been raped. The police were called. She was medically examined. The 'boys', as they called themselves, were charged and each lined up a lawyer.

I was chosen because I was female, so my new client, Snake, told me. The theory was that jurors would think that no woman would act for a rapist and so he would be acquitted. 'Good, as long as it's not because I'm competent. We couldn't have that,' I snarled. The sarcasm was lost on my audience.

Snake's instructions (instructions are what a client tells a lawyer) were basically as follows: 'She was askin' for it,' and, 'Don't worry mate, I've done plenty of gaol and I can do it again.' Roughly translated, this seemed to be a plea of not guilty and a vote of no-confidence.

As a beginner in the Supreme Court, I was reassured by the fact that there would be three other lawyers. Each of the four accused men had his own lawyer. For me, as well as for the clients, there was safety in numbers. I would be third cab off the rank, as my client's name was third in alphabetical order, which for an inexperienced lawyer was a pretty good position. My biggest job was not to ask questions which would mess things up for the others. Everyone planned to work together as their clients' interests were all the same. What was good for one was good for the other. A bit like the three Musketeers, except there were four of them.

The big day arrived.

I arrived at court early and made my way to the women barristers' robing room. The male barristers had a lovely timber panelled room with wooden lockers for their daily clothes. The women had to share a minuscule vinyl-tiled room with the cleaners' supplies and a toilet which was also used by many of the female court staff. There was often a queue for the loo, especially at five to 10 when I was late for court. I took my red eighties-style shoulder-padded jacket off, and shrugged on my jabot, my black bar jacket (a fitted short jacket) and my black gown. On with the itchy horsehair wig, a quick look in the mirror, and the show was on the road.

Down to the dungeons to see my client, who had handed himself in to the police in the detention area earlier in the morning, as he was required to do by the terms of his bail.

The detention cells were reached by a flight of dark wooden stairs leading down directly from the dock. Cigarettes were officially unavailable, but unofficially given by guards to prisoners to keep them quiet. (They almost kept another client of mine permanently quiet when he was set alight by another prisoner in the rear of a locked, armoured prisoner transport van.)

My client was wearing his best, least dirty denim trousers and had trimmed his beard, or so he said: it still looked pretty scruffy to me. He stank of cigarettes and beer, having arrived at court directly from a 'last supper'.

In those days, once a trial started, the accused would be locked up in prison each night for the duration to avoid the chance of them running into a juror, accidentally or otherwise. It was therefore not unusual for a client to turn up still drunk from the night before, realising that he may not be in a position to drink again for quite some time, especially if he was convicted.

Snake seemed to be pretty confident, much more confident than I was feeling. I felt sick with nerves. He wished me good luck.

Knickers?

Back upstairs, I looked through the brass porthole window in the green baize door to make sure I was about to enter the correct courtroom. The other lawyers were already there, arrayed behind the red leather bar table like so many crows on a washing line. Upstairs, in an area like the dress circle at a movie theatre or playhouse, with a view down over the courtroom, the public galleries were packed.

The prosecutor made a flamboyant speech, emphasising the more sordid and sleazy aspects of the evening, and the fact that all four accused belong to the same 'bikie gang'. The first witness for the prosecution was the complainant. She walked meekly to the witness box, accompanied by a kindly middle-aged lady, her 'support person'. She (the complainant) was wearing a floral dress in shades of pink and mauve, a neat navy blue blazer, low-heeled navy blue court shoes and a white Alice band in her hair. At the pub, this young lady had been wearing a thin singlet-style dress, a torn denim jacket and no underwear. She had definitely taken lessons from someone about how to dress in court.

I did pretty well asking a very few, but mostly sensible, questions on behalf of my client. The other lawyers had asked most of what needed to be asked already. They had been a bit nervous about me cutting my teeth on 'their' trial, but were starting to relax. Unfortunately, the last lawyer, whose questions followed mine, seemed to have left his common sense at home.

It was a jury trial, and he was looking for a 'killer' question designed to really impress the jury. The idea is that the jurors would rise as one, and shout to the judge, 'Enough already! Let these poor misunderstood upright gentlemen go free! And compensate them while you are at it!' And here it is, the triumphant question to top all questions: 'Are you wearing any knickers today?'

What earthly point was there in asking that? One of two things could have happened: she could have said 'Yes', or she could have said 'No'.

If she had said 'Yes', what was this lawyer going to do, ask her to prove it? 'Young lady, please lift your skirt for the jury.' I don't think so! Obviously, the question would have got him nowhere, and would have been offensive as well.

If she had said 'No,' it would then reduce the impact

upon the jury of her wearing no knickers at the pub. If she was prepared to wear no knickers at court, perhaps it wasn't that significant. Maybe she wasn't the cheap slut he was trying to paint her as, after all.

This is exactly what happened. She said, 'No, I used to live in a very hot climate and got used to the idea of not wearing any knickers and so have never worn them since.'

If I had been on the jury, I would have thought this lawyer's approach was just plain silly and offensive. I would have thought that if the best he could do in defence of his client was to ask a gratuitous question like that, then his client couldn't really have had much of a defence and must have been guilty.

The trial went rapidly downhill after that and the four men were convicted after the jury deliberated for seven hours. It was a measure of our misery that we viewed a seven-hour deliberation as something of a victory. The defence lawyers consoled each other with mutterings of, 'Well, at least we made them think.'

I trudged down the timber stairs to see my client after the unanimous jury verdict, a little fearful about his reaction. My client, bless his heart, just said, 'Never mind, mate, you did your best!'

It is now close to 20 years later. He has been in trouble since, but never in such trouble. Whenever he is misunderstood by members of our police, he returns to my tender care.

Anatomy lesson

I have been critical of the lawyer for Bikie #4 for asking a silly question, but I must admit I have often asked exceptionally stupid questions and only sometimes got away with them.

One of the stupidest questions I ever asked was in an armed robbery trial where I was attempting to suggest that the female witness (the estranged girlfriend of one of the alleged robbers) was getting a bit carried away with her evidence in the witness box. I asked, 'Have you ever had any acting training?' I realised as soon as I asked that it was a classic smart alec question which could only backfire on me. There must be a god for lawyers, however, because she answered, 'Yes, as a matter of fact I'm an actress.' I looked smug, as if this was the answer I had been expecting all along. After the trial, I found out that her only dramatic experience was walking round shopping centres in a yellow chicken suit advertising some form of fried chicken.

Sometimes there are questions which simply can't be asked. In one trial, there was a dispute as to who was the subject of a stack of pornographic pictures. Again, there was a wronged girlfriend in the picture, so to speak. She found these pictures on her ex-boyfriend's coffee table when she went snooping after he had moved out of his home and started living with someone else. She said they were of herself, and he said they were of the new girlfriend.

Unfortunately, the photographer had only taken aspects of anatomy that were of interest to him (or her, I suppose). Let me just say that this did not include the face, nor any other obviously identifying features. What was I supposed to do? Get the new and old girlfriends in and ask them to let the jury compare? Again, I don't think so.

The spurned lady did offer to undergo a medical examination to see whether the bits in the photograph could be identified as hers. I suppose at least that was better than the alternative—a line-up. Police will sometimes use other police or people off the street if they are willing to take part in a line-up or identity parade, but I can't see anybody, police or otherwise, being willing to take part in that sort of exercise when one is identifying pudenda.

The same problem came up in a trial where my client was alleged to have had an incestuous relationship with his stepdaughter. I find it a curious human trait that people will persist in taking photographs and leaving evidence around for police to find! This gentleman, and I use that term very loosely indeed, seemed to photograph everything. In fact he videotaped everything. It was in the days when home video cameras had just started to become affordable.

This man was a real enthusiast. He had discovered all these special effects of his camera. Freeze-frame was a particular favourite. He videotaped his own ejaculation in freeze-frame, which was probably one of the most repulsive things I have ever seen. He also liked to urinate into a wine glass, with a rose added for special effect.

In this case, the perennial question came up about just who was the subject of certain video footage. The accused had filmed the subject of his interest only from the neck down, the face being clearly of no interest to him. The talented female in the videotape was able to blow bubbles from her bits. The prosecutor and I discussed whether the jury should be shown this footage so that they could make up their minds who it was, the issue being whether it was mother or daughter, as if it had been the mother it would have been quite legal, although quite disgusting.

Obviously, we were very reluctant to go down this path. But if we did not, how on earth was the jury supposed to decide which of the two women it was? There was no practical answer to this. Luckily for everyone concerned, including the lawyers, the judge and the poor jury, I managed to persuade this man to plead guilty so we were all spared.

Eeew

Usually allegations of sexual intercourse without consent relate to men doing the deed with women. However, it is not unheard of for men to allege that other men have raped them. One young man alleged that he had been at a drunken dinner party and had consumed a huge amount of alcohol with a group of friends. They had all repaired back to the house of one of the group to drink on, and one by one the young people had gone to bed, being far too sensible to drive home in their condition. The alleged victim said he had gone to sleep on a mattress on the floor and woke up to find my client withdrawing, having just finished having sexual intercourse with him. The alleged victim said that he had not consented to this happening. My client said it didn't happen at all, though he did share the mattress with the other person.

Now, tactics in jury selection are a bit of a black art. Nobody really knows much about what sort of jurors are good for what sorts of trials. These days people suggest that the defence should choose teachers on trials where someone is said to have had sexual contact with a child, because they may be sympathetic to the accused, thinking 'There but for the grace of God go I.' I don't know how true this is, and no offence I hope will be taken by our teachers. The point is that many of them are rightfully fearful of misguided or unfounded allegations.

In this trial, with the specific allegation that had been made, I got as many men on the jury as I possibly could. The whole defence revolved around, 'What? You mean he only became aware he was being raped as the other guy was pulling out? *Surely* he would feel it going in?' I swear that as the relevant evidence was being presented, and as I was addressing them along these lines at the end, the men on the jury were literally squirming in their seats.

One of the main pieces of incriminating evidence in this trial, particularly considering that my client claimed there had been no intercourse at all, was a hair (one of the alleged victim's own) which had been found quite a long way inside the nether regions of the alleged victim. The question from the prosecution point of view was, how else could this hair have got there, other than by intercourse? My suggestion to that, which did not find much favour with the prosecution expert, was that he could have swallowed it. Well, I thought that was a good idea. The jury acquitted on one charge and convicted on the other, so I have no idea whether my good idea found favour or not.

His own worst enemy

Another of my clients was supposed to have raped a fellow inmate in prison. He was quite happy to tell me that he was heterosexual, but he did have sex with men in prison. It seems this somehow didn't count, as it was in a custodial setting. Needs must and all that.

This case came up for its first run in the days when we had preliminary hearings which were just that, hearings to decide whether the matter should go to trial at all. This one didn't. Here's why:

The 'victim' was in the witness box. I was asking him questions.

'So, tell us about a typical day in prison. What time do you get up? What time do you go to bed? What happens of an evening?'

'I knew you were going to ask me about what happens of an evening. I take my medication, OK?'

'What was your medication for?' (Me having had no idea he was on any form of medication.)

'It was lithium, OK? Wanna make something of that? Just because I take lithium doesn't mean I'm crazy.' (I happened to know from several murder trials where insanity was the defence that lithium carbonate is a common drug taken to control the symptoms of schizophrenia.)

'No-one has suggested you're crazy, but what was it for?'

'I'm bipolar, all right?' (bipolar disorder is sometimes known as manic depression), 'and I know what you're going to ask me next.'

(Me now asking totally random questions with no idea what the answers were going to be except that I had a strong feeling that the answers were likely to be good for the defence.) 'What am I going to ask you next?'

'You're going to say that I made all this up so I can get a transfer to another prison.'

'Why am I going to say that?' (There is a 'rule' among lawyers that you should never ask a question you do not know the answer to, for fear it may blow up in your face. I was dicing with death-for-lawyers by heading down this path but feeling pretty good nonetheless.)

'Every time I get too deep into my gambling debts I ask for a transfer, but that's not why I am doing it this time.'

'Are you going to ask for a transfer?' (I didn't even know that.)

'Yes.' (Now I am having another out-of-body experience. Things are going right: righter than right! It's a miracle! I think I will try walking on red-hot coals next.)

'Do you have gambling debts right now?' (I'm on a roll.)

'Yes.'

'What else am I going to ask you?'

At this point, the 'victim' turned to the magistrate and asked, 'Can I keep telling her stuff, your Holiness?'

'Yes,' was the reply from on high, 'but you are your own worst enemy.'

I leapt in, 'Oh no, your Worship, I'm perfectly happy for him to continue telling me "stuff".'

'I bet you are.'

With all the clues this 'victim' (I was actually starting to think of him as an accused) had given me on a silver platter without any effort on my part, I thought I would do some more digging. As a result of said digging, I managed to get my hands on the medical records from the prison health service. Among a veritable mountain of useful stuff were nurses' notes describing him as an inveterate liar who would manipulate and say anything to get his own way. Jackpot!

Not surprisingly, the prosecution dropped the case soon afterwards and my client never went to trial proper. Home free (well, still in gaol, but without the bonus time a conviction on this case would have given him).

Always do your homework

No matter how much homework a lawyer does, and no matter how certain they are that they know the answers to the questions which are likely to be asked, things sometimes fall apart totally unexpectedly. I watched a trial where there were three people, all jointly accused of murder. As a matter of common sense, they were either all not guilty, or all guilty. The defence lawyers had pooled their efforts, probably partly because they were all working for legal aid fees, which have traditionally been almost less than nothing. One of the defence lawyers had organised a forensic pathologist to give evidence. All the defence lawyers expected this evidence to help them.

The pathologist gave his evidence, which did indeed favour the defence.

The prosecutor stood up, with a barely concealed smirk on his face. I don't blame him: if I had had the ammunition he had, I would have had trouble not laughing outright.

'Doctor, do you always tell the truth?'

'I'm telling the truth in court today.' (I was already starting to get worried.)

'Doctor, are you sure?'

'Yes, I'm sure.' (Surely he would not say this if his conscience was not clear? And yet at the same time, I was getting more and more worried. The jury was sitting up straight, and hanging on every word.)

'Well, Doctor,' (enormously long pause), 'is it not the

case that you are currently serving a suspended term of imprisonment for nine counts of perjury?'

For the first time, I realised what the term 'gobsmacked' meant. The jurors' mouths were hanging open. There was a seemingly interminable pause before everyone recovered and went on. This pause was probably no more than 30 seconds, just long enough for me to look around the room and realise that it was almost in freeze-frame. No-one had moved. No-one had said anything. No-one could breathe.

The prosecutor stood there, waiting for an answer, positively orgasmic. It was clearly a highlight of his career. As it happened, the perjury was nothing to do with evidence this man had given in a professional capacity but rather something to do with tax or family law or one of those problems that seems to encourage even the most law-abiding and conservative citizen to lie.

There was another potential murder on the cards that day. The other two defence lawyers who had been counting on their colleague to save the day were, I believe, making hurried plans to kill him.

Honesty the best policy

Sometimes, rarely but effectively, a client's criminal background works for him, not against him.

Usually in criminal jury trials there is a rule that a person's criminal record is 'off-limits' unless the accused has brought up the subject of character by saying they are as pure as the driven snow, or have accused prosecution witnesses of horrible things, thus suggesting that they are people of bad character. This rule came about because of the theory that juries will be unfairly prejudiced if they get to hear about a person's record when that person is on trial.

Sometimes this rule places the defence in a very difficult position, when as a necessary part of the defence they are forced to attack a prosecution witness's character.

An Aboriginal client was charged with sexually assaulting a white woman. He had a criminal record which could be measured by the metre. His story was that he had gone to this lady's house to purchase heroin, that she had invited him to join her in bed, and that after they had had their way with each other and she was sound asleep, he took his opportunity, stole the heroin and ran. He said that she was making up the allegation of sexual assault to get back at him for the theft of heroin.

To defend him, I had to suggest that she was a drug dealer which meant he would have to admit that he was a heroin user and a thief. My problem with this was that she had no criminal record whatsoever. He did, in a major way. He was black. She was white.

There was nothing for it: the problem had to be tackled head-on. Rather than have the prosecution bring up my client's criminal record in cross-examination, I thought we may as well deal with it immediately and take some of the wind out of the prosecution's sails.

I asked him: 'Tell the members of the jury, do you have a criminal record?'

'Yes, I do.'

'Is this it?' (producing an enormously long concertina of paper).

'Yes, it is.'

'What's on it?'

'Mostly burglary, stealing and drug offences.'

'Have you ever been on trial in a criminal court?'

'No.'

'Why not?'

'Because I done all them other things so I pleaded guilty.'

'Why are you having a trial now?'

'Because I didn't do this one.'

'Do you have any sexual offences on your record?'

'No, I do drugs and stuff, but I don't do sex.'

Despite his undeniably poor character, the difference in their skin colour, and the fact that I had to call someone without a criminal record a drug dealer, the jury took a very short time to unanimously acquit him. Honesty really was the best policy in this instance.

Ringbark Robbie

Many of my clients lived in a world very different from mine, with different rules and different morals. I had to keep reminding myself of this. When I did, it put their wrongdoings into a different context.

Ringbark Robbie bore a scar around his entire body midway up his chest. The scar was inflicted due to a drug debt. He was inordinately fond of showing it off to visitors.

He and his family were a bit like Rumpole's Timson family. They kept me in business. Whoever was out of gaol at the time was getting into trouble and I was kept busy trying to keep them out, or appeal when they went in.

On this occasion, Robbie had been charged with aggravated sexual assault. He had managed to get himself accused of not just having sex with a 15-year-old, but also with threatening to cut her nipples off with his knife. As you do.

This sounds utterly horrifying. And it was. However, it can be put into some sort of context. The girl concerned was a distant relative. She worked as a prostitute in a brothel run by her mother. Robbie would usually turn up on a Friday night for a freebie, and generally get it. On this particular Friday night he turned up extremely drunk and both mother and daughter refused his usual request for a freebie. He was not in the least happy and it was at this point that he made the threats.

He had sex with the daughter and stayed the night, as he usually did. The next morning, the entire happy family was around the kitchen table eating their Weeties, when Mum said, 'Right, Robbie, I'm telling the cops on you because you shouldn't have turned up drunk.' Not because of the threats, mind you, and not because of the intercourse with her daughter, but because of the social faux pas of being drunk. Robbie pleaded guilty, did his time and was released. He now lives at the same brothel.

Prison Greens

'Prison greens' is the name given to the unmistakable clothes male prisoners in Western Australian jails wear. The white pyjamas with rows of black arrows are considered a bit passé these days. The colour of the modern outfit is a dreadful bottle green (reminds me of my first school uniform) and the style is best described as shapeless: T-shirt and tracksuit bottoms, with a windcheater for cooler weather. Bottle green thongs in summer, white trainers in winter (no manufacturer has yet made these in bottle green). I should add for the enlightenment of international readers that in Australia thongs are footwear, not underwear. Female prisoners have an equally revolting maroon outfit.

Many prisoners show their individuality by the addition of tattoos, often done inside prison by people of doubtful artistic ability using doubtful tools and ink from a ballpoint pen. You have the tattooed tears under one eye (said to represent how many individuals you have killed), the words 'LOVE' and 'HATE' on the knuckles (very popular among the older crims), and the names of various loved or used-to-be-loved ones. Pretty stupid really, as those same tattoos are invaluable in identifying bank robbers, rapists and sundry other crooks when they are released and return to their old ways. Police and victims do, however, appreciate the thoughtfulness of criminals in voluntarily 'branding' themselves.

I used to think that if a criminal were smart, he would not get caught. I have since come to realise that for career criminals, getting caught is a statistical concept: the more crime you commit, the more likely you are to get caught sometime. They view getting caught and a stint in prison as part of the price of doing business, a bit like taxes. A few months or a year away from the maddening pace of juggling four or five telephones in one's drug-dealing business is almost welcomed: a chance to get fit, eat properly, catch up with overdue reading, learn new skills (some legal, some not), and, importantly, fit in some serious networking, making contacts who will be useful on the outside.

Certainly prison greens DO stand out in a crowd, as I discovered to my detriment one memorable day. I had assumed this would be one of my easier jobs. Quite routine, really.

Neil's vermin problem

Neil was a chap who, in the great Australian tradition, was into 'self-help'. Just as most Australian men will not stop to ask directions, Neil did not stop to think of a more legal way of sorting out his particular problem.

About 10 years before, Neil had lived in a neat little house (a triple-fronted brick venereal, as Dame Edna would say) in a neat little suburb with a neat little vegetable garden. He was a single man. His wife had left him a couple of years earlier, after the children had all left home. It seems she wanted more excitement than the weekly trip to the 'dogs' (greyhound races, for the uninitiated) and the 'all-you-can-eat buffet' at the local club. He was a large man, tall and tending to a little flab, but kept himself neat and tidy (after all, you never know when romance might strike), with a sandy trimmed moustache, a sandy tending to grey comb-over kept in place by a sprinkling of Californian Poppy hair oil, and a nice beige cardigan knitted by his elderly mum, with leather patches on the elbows. What a benign, conservative picture Neil presented.

Neil had not always been a pillar of rectitude, however. In his youth Neil had misbehaved a fair bit and had spent some months in a juvenile training institution where he acquired some of the aforementioned homemade tattoos and a certain wariness of attitude around police. He had, though, put his wild youth behind him and had held down a series of steady jobs for his entire adult life, ranging from storeman at Woolworth's to clerking at the local asphalting company. Now, nearing retirement age, Neil had acquired a problem.

Neil had a problem with his neighbours: they were neighbours from hell. Their house was overrun by cockroaches and rats and there were other signs of neglect. There seemed to be a floating population of relatives and friends moving in and out, certainly more at any one time than the place was built to handle. The drinking would start about nine in the morning and continue unabated until about four the following morning, when the occupants seemed to pass out briefly. For a few hours peace would return to the suburban street. Then it would start all over again. If it wasn't the neighbours screaming and howling at all hours of the day and night, it was the sounds of cursing and bottles breaking. Worst of all, even the cockroaches and rats in the neighbours' house couldn't stand it anymore and decided they were going to move, and (yes, you guessed it) they moved into Neil's home.

Neil fretted. Neil stewed. Neil obsessed. Neil was resourceful. He would show the world that he wasn't the milksop appearances might have suggested. He had a solution. There was a way to get rid of the cockroaches, the rats and the neighbours in one go.

A plan was hatched. Neil waited. Week after week he waited. The moment had to be just right.

Every second Thursday was pension day, when money next door was temporarily plentiful. Alcohol was also plentiful, and the racket was at its loudest. On one of these Thursday evenings the house next door suddenly went quiet: Neil's neighbours were at the pub buying more supplies. Neil decided the time was right. *Carpe diem*, he thought to himself, seize the day! (He had seen the Robin Williams movie.) He decided to take advantage of the temporary lull in hostilities. He donned his dark trackpants, a dark jumper over his pyjamas and, with a fine sense of drama, an old black stocking of his ex-wife's over his head. His plan of many weeks was ready to be carried out.

It was a moonless night, and the only witnesses to

what was about to happen were the cicadas chirping their evening gossip. Barefoot, a rusted chrome torch in his hand with the beam close to his feet, he moved swiftly from his back door and down his lovingly concreted path to the back shed. In this shed the meticulous Neil kept all the things which made him a man: his leaf blower, his lawnmower, his hand tools hung carefully on a pin board where their outlines had been drawn. Arrayed along the back of his work bench was an assortment of tins, jars and bottles containing a range of nails, screws, and various liquids, including leftover paint (might come in handy one day), turpentine, methylated spirits, and petrol.

Hands shaking and heart thumping with rage and excitement, Neil poured several of the volatile liquids into an old four-litre ice-cream container and stirred them around with a piece of dowel. Eyes watering from the fumes, he carefully poured the resulting mixture into a battered green jerry can and made his way through the hole in the paling fence between the two properties.

Dodging the broken glass in the neighbours' dusty back yard, he made his way to their back screen door. It was locked, but there was a hole in the rusted flywire just right for putting a hand through to undo the sliding bolt. The door proper behind it was wide open. Neil moved quickly through the house, shining his torch into each room, checking in case a paralytically drunk occupant had been left behind while the rest went to the pub.

No-one.

Neil poured the contents of the jerry can over the ancient sofa in the living room, lit a match, and, quite deliberately, burnt the house down. Mission accomplished. No more rats, no more cockroaches, and no more neighbours.

But ... Neil was not the sharpest pencil in the box. He had boasted to his mates in the pub the night before about what he was going to do, and after he had done the deed he went back to the pub and boasted again. Not only that, but while the house was burning down he set up a tripod and videotaped himself standing proudly in front of it. He kept the tape well hidden (!) under his mattress. He left the jerry can next door, covered in his greasy fingerprints. In case that was not enough, the can also had his name and telephone number scratched into the base. He had motive, means and opportunity. Identifying the perpetrator was not one of the more challenging jobs the arson squad had ever faced.

As Neil had been careful enough to ensure that the neighbours were actually out before he spread the petrol and set it alight, and perhaps because the police had some sympathy for him, he was not charged with attempted murder. It was just a mild case of arson.

Neil' next move

Neil had not been in any trouble with the law for many years—not so much as a parking ticket. Arson was reasonably seriously regarded by the legislators and so was reserved for a judge to deal with, not a magistrate. However, everyone has to appear in front of a magistrate on their way to the higher courts. The police and the magistrate before whom Neil first appeared on his way to that higher court did not think he was a flight risk, so he was allowed out on bail on his own promise (with a $10,000 guarantee attached) to reappear in court in a few weeks, after he had received some legal advice. I don't know what that advice was, or even if he had any, but Neil did not reappear in court. He was 'on the run'.

Neil's idea of going on the run was to move to the east coast of Australia, take up with a lovely lady he met at the bingo, get a steady job and save up enough money to buy a caravan and become one of Australia's floating population of 'grey nomads', heading south for the summer and north for winter, or trundling their way around Australia, usually in an anticlockwise direction. Hardly a threat to the fabric of our society, so long as the neighbours behaved themselves.

Neil spent close to 10 years out of Western Australia. Life was going remarkably well until, on one of his weekly boys' nights out, Neil's tongue got the better of him. One of the 'boys' was a retired police officer who rather disloyally rang his mates in the west with the tip-off. Neil was unceremoniously uprooted from his settled and cosy life, forced to tell his new wife something of his past, appeared in the Parramatta Court for an extradition hearing, and then found himself on a plane back to Perth between two hungover West Australian police officers.

Sometimes the State budget would allow officers to travel to collect a wanted criminal from interstate where he had been located, sometimes not. It depended on the seriousness of the crime. Neil's arson was borderline, but they could hardly ignore a tip-off from a respected colleague.

An informal entertainment budget was established in each State to show these visiting officers a good time. A side note: it used to be said by certain West Australian police in the 'bad old days' that 'an extradition's not over till you vomit'. Unfortunately for the visitors, they usually had to give evidence in court about just why this miscreant should be extradited before they could take him out of the State he had been located in. I have cross-examined such officers on many occasions and found them to be incredibly easy targets, mainly because they had been out the evening before with their interstate colleagues and were not particularly well when they fronted court. Having said that, the case for extradition is usually a rubber-stamp job—close to watertight and with a sympathetic magistrate—so usually these officers just had to show up and not throw up.

Times have changed. The Police Force or Service or whatever it is currently called (it keeps changing), is a much cleaner operation, but if you ask me some of the fun has gone, too.

Honour among thieves

Back to Neil: on his first court appearance the day after he had been returned involuntarily to Perth, he pleaded guilty. Because he had not seen a lawyer, the sentencing was deferred until he found someone who would speak on his behalf. Due to the fact that he had 'done a runner', there was no way any magistrate or judge was going to grant him bail, so he spent his time in a Western Australian prison waiting to be dealt with by the courts.

At the time, I was 'flavour of the month' at Fremantle Prison. This is a phenomenon well known to criminal defence lawyers, usually resulting from having a satisfied customer inside the prison. Often this is someone undoubtedly guilty, who received a lesser sentence due to their lawyer's real or imagined eloquence in pleading their case (may the best sob story win). More often this was down to sheer good luck—an under-prepared prosecutor or drawing the right judge. In any case, such a result means a rush of clients that lasts between three and six months. Someone gave Neil the hot tip, and he asked me to represent him for his 'plea in mitigation' (the aforementioned sob story).

My first meeting with Neil was in the depressing surroundings of the old prison. This prison is now a tourist attraction, offering ghost tours as part of the history of the old port town of Fremantle, just south of Perth. I've never been able to go back there as a tourist. There are too many other memories associated with the prison for me.

Back when it housed prisoners, Fremantle Prison, which is built largely of stone, was a dank and miserable place. Located in the middle of the port city of Fremantle, south of Perth, it was surrounded by ten-metre high stone walls topped with razor wire. The walls did not present much of a barrier to those intent on delivering drugs and other contraband to prisoners. If the delivery would fit into a tennis ball, a master craftsman would open up a split in its side, and the ball was simply thrown over the walls and collected by the recipient.

Neil did not misbehave in this manner. He kept his nose clean and waited for his day of reckoning.

The place was designed for bad dudes of generations ago, who were less well nourished and therefore much shorter than today's prisoners. Neil ducked his head as he came through the door into the Official Visits Area and greeted me with a clammy shake of his large hand. He sat on the not-very-sturdy used-to-be-white plastic chair (the type gracing probably millions of Australian backyards) and started to talk. I sat on the swivel typist's chair across the small grey laminex table, looked and listened.

On his knuckles he bore the standard 'LOVE' and 'HATE' tattoos, and on his face he bore a look of abject misery. 'All I want to do is to get back to me missus. I'm pleading guilty. I done it and there's no two ways about it. I still want to go around Australia while I can. Everything

I've got is tied up in the caravan and me life savings. I worked all me life, except for those few months when I was a young tacker. Please, Miss, just get me out of here and get me back home. I don't fit in here now: don't have any truck with those young druggies. They'd sell their own grandma and they don't have any morals.'

I took his point. The younger generation of criminal certainly lacked the code of conduct possessed by the old school. There used to be a type of honour among thieves. There were certain things which were just beyond the pale: these included harming children in any way, and informing on another crim. Swift and vicious jailhouse justice has always awaited those who transgress in these ways.

Loyalty to one's lawyer was generally part of this code. A venerable criminal lawyer of my acquaintance once told me that his car had been stolen. When the thief was finally caught and told whose car it was, the response was, 'If I'd of known it was his I would never of touched it.' The thief was, perhaps for the first time in his career, genuinely remorseful.

Neil's day in court

As Neil wanted to get it over and done with as soon as possible, we were in court within a couple of weeks. Court 56, Central Law Courts. Soporific. Ugly. Squeaky seats with more suspicious stains. I was doing my best to tug upon the heartstrings of the judge. He was a judge I had appeared before many times, and I harboured a belief that he still retained heartstrings. I was doing my standard plea in mitigation. Translated, this means 'Please don't throw the book at him, judge, because (a) he only did it to feed his starving children, (b) he wasn't breastfed when he was a baby, and (c) he is really, really, REALLY sorry and it was a moment of madness.'

As I went on, I started picking up on the judge's mood. I'm not sure how to explain this apparent psychic ability, but most lawyers who have been around for a few years develop it. It involves reading non-verbal cues such as rolling of the eyeballs ('Pull the other one: it plays Jingle Bells'); picking up a pen and starting to write ('I have made up my mind so you may as well sit down and shut up'); nodding with varying degrees of vigour ('I agree, so quit while you are ahead'); shaking of the head in the general direction of the jury while a witness is giving evidence ('Should we charge this person with perjury now or later?'). One day I will get together with a psychologist and write *Fordham's Patented Judge Mood Divining Manual*, sell it to all the new lawyers and make my fortune.

I had not thought there was even a possibility that the judge would not lock him up for an extended period of time. Arson is a serious offence and someone could have been badly hurt if things had gone wrong. The cue this judge was giving was pretty unmistakeable, however. He said, 'I suppose, Ms Fordham, you're going to ask me not to imprison him in light of his conduct since the offence. After all, he has experienced the rigours of prison life for the past couple of weeks, and his recent history would suggest he is not likely to reoffend.' Being reasonably quick on the uptake that day, I hastened to assure the judge that this was exactly what I had been aiming at (even though the truth was I had not in fact even considered it.) My mother always said 'a little white lie never hurt anyone'. I almost congratulated the judge on his perspicacity, but thought that may have been going too far.

So it was fairly obvious that, after 10 years of leading a blameless life (this is Neil I'm talking about, not the judge, about whose life I knew very little at the time), the judge was inclined not to imprison him. Just before lunchtime, the judge interrupted what I was saying to announce, 'That is all very well, Ms Fordham, but what about his bail? There was a $10,000 promise to reappear in court and he broke that promise. He'll have to pay up before I even consider releasing him.'

After a hurried conference with Neil, I went back to the judge with an offer: Neil would give up all his life savings—which, coincidentally, amounted to just over $10,000, and which were sitting in the bank ready for his around-Australia trip. You might think that would be the end of it, but no! Bureaucracy, or security, or a combination of both, was about to present a major hurdle.

Neil was still in custody. He was going to stay in custody until the $10,000 was paid. He had the money in the bank. He had a card which would permit him to withdraw the money. This card was in his belongings at the prison. The prison officers were not prepared to get the card and withdraw the money as there were rules against conducting banking transactions for prisoners. They were not prepared to get the card and give it to me as this also, for some reason, constituted conducting a banking transaction. They were prepared to take it from his belongings at the prison and would give it to him at court, but they would not let him give it to me. This somehow also was a banking transaction.

The judge's 'solution'

It seemed the only person who could get the money was Neil, but he was in custody. He was locked in a cell in the custody area of the courts complex when not in court, and while in court he was accompanied by two officers, ready to spring into action if it looked as though he were about to run off. He could not go to the bank, and given his past performance, bail was not really an option.

All these difficulties were ventilated in court with all parties becoming more and more frustrated until a strange expression crossed the judge's face. Were I less charitable, I would have called it an evil expression, but let's just call it 'strange'.

His Honour: 'Ms Fordham, I have the solution.'

Me: 'Yes, your Honour?'

His Honour: 'You are an officer of this court, are you not?' All lawyers are 'officers of the court' which is generally taken to mean that they are especially reliable and trustworthy, and have some form of official status the nature of which I have yet to figure out.

Me: 'Yes, your Honour.'

His Honour: 'Obviously what we need to do is to get this prisoner to the bank.'

Me: 'Yes, your Honour.'

His Honour: 'I'm not prepared to release him from custody until he pays the $10,000 he owes for breaching his bail.'

Me: (injecting some variety but thinking, 'Where is this going? I don't like the sound of it at all.) 'No, your Honour.'

His Honour: 'Here is the plan. I am placing him in your custody and you are to take him to the bank. The custody centre officers are to hand him over to you. You will accompany him. He will withdraw the money and return with it.'

Me: (speechless)

His Honour: 'Well, is that a problem?'

Me: 'No, your Honour.' (This was the second outright lie of the morning. In my defence I can only say I was in deep shock. I had never heard of such a thing. I did not think the judge had the power to do it, but what did I know? He was the judge, I was not.)

Up I went to the custody area on the fifth floor. I stood

outside the door waiting for the officer watching the closed circuit television monitor to buzz me in. The bell which used to operate from the outside to alert the officers that someone was wanting to enter had been disconnected some years before by officers fed up with relatives and friends wanting to pay social visits to the prisoners. On this occasion, the door buzzed almost immediately. I pushed it and made my way down the narrow corridor where I waited for the inner door to open.

I was greeted by perhaps six officers doing their best to control their laughter. I can only assume they had been forewarned by the judge's associate, as they seemed quite willing, even eager, to hand him over to me. I had hoped they would refuse. No such luck.

Neil came out through an internal door ceremoniously unlocked by the custody officer. I had forgotten just how tall he was. He was extraordinarily tall, wearing his prison greens, with his green prison thongs (footwear, not G-strings, remember) on his feet, and the familiar tattoos on his knuckles. I noticed for the first time that he also had tattoos on his toes. I did not get close enough to read them. I was having a sort of out-of-body experience: I could stand back and see what was happening, but I did not believe it.

How was I supposed to control him? Have I mentioned my own height? (162 centimetres and shrinking.) No handcuffs. No pepper spray for me to use. No shackles. Nothing. What on earth was I going to do if he decided to run away? Or take me hostage? Ask him nicely to 'Please come back?' As I left with 'my' prisoner, I heard the barely suppressed giggles erupt into guffaws.

Along the long corridor on the fifth floor we walked. Police officers waiting to give evidence in court looked at us strangely. My lawyer colleagues milling about in the same corridors looked at us even more strangely. Into the lift. Packed with lawyers, court groupies, happily no journalists, and several people with evident alcohol and personal hygiene problems. Out of the main doors of the courthouse and into the main street of Perth.

In charge of the Jolly Green Giant

It was just on 1pm. It seemed to me that with every step we took towards the bank, Neil grew taller and I grew shorter. Anyone who was anyone was in that street and staring at us. The prison greens, far from being bottle green, now seemed to fluoresce. It was as if there was a large sign above his head pointing down saying 'ESCAPED PRISONER' and a sign above mine saying 'HOSTAGE', or 'STUPID LAWYER', or 'FAILED PERSON'. My mind was racing, trying to work out just what I was going to do if he took off. I think the solution I came up with was 'nothing'. That's it! That's what I'll do! Nothing. All those years at law school. All that training. All that court experience. And the best I can do is … nothing. Career? What career? Did you know I used to be a lawyer?

The experience is permanently engraved on my brain. I

can see it now, like a very bad movie which replays without warning. Bravely Neil struts into the bank and (cringing) I sidle in with him. Up to the counter. The teller looks at him. A glazed but terrified expression forms on her face, as she looks at me and then back at him, clearly recognising the significance of Neil's garb.

I squeak, 'We'd like $10,000 please. In cash.' (That's right, the judge wanted cash.) The teller's finger moves slowly towards the duress alarm just under the counter. I gabble, 'It's OK, I'm a lawyer' (as if that would help), and somehow I manage to convince her to call her boss, who in turn I somehow (no idea at all how: my brain has blocked out this part of the trauma) convince of the legitimacy of this banking transaction.

The cash is produced and is counted out. Neil reaches for it, and for the first time my common sense returns. I say, 'I'll take that.' Neil does not object but, clearly realising that it is now only a matter of time before he is 'home free', starts getting a bit cheeky. He leans on the counter, and with a conspiratorial chuckle says to the teller, 'I don't know, you work hard all your life for a few bucks—the next thing you know the bloody missus takes it all.'

'Shut up shut up shut up,' I snarled between clenched teeth. 'Let's just get back and hand the money over.' So, we started the long sideshow trek back to court.

It was only about 200 metres, but trust me, it was a long, long way. The bank was midway between the courthouse and the police prosecutions office. Lawyers had their offices all around the area. There seemed to be a prearranged plan for everybody I had ever wanted to impress to gather in that street on that day. And they could all tell I was walking up the road with an enormous prisoner (and don't forget the tattoos).

We reached the door of the courthouse. It was only 1.30pm. Court did not reconvene until 2.15pm.

'I need a smoke,' said Neil, cheekier by the minute. 'Too bad,' I said. 'I don't smoke and don't have any cigarettes.'

'Ah yes,' he chortled, 'but we've got money and we don't have to be back for at least half an hour.'

Off we went again, to the newsagent to buy cigarettes and matches. There is something very strange about standing next to an arsonist and purchasing matches. But I did it.

We stood outside the doors of the courthouse, positioned so that every single person entering or leaving the building through that entrance had to walk within 15 centimetres of us as the Jolly Green Giant smoked. At 2.10pm we entered the building, I handed him back to his gaolers in the custody area, we went back into court (but only after I made up the difference of the price of the packet of cigarettes and the lighter to deposit the full $10,000) and, as predicted, the judge released him.

Aside from an overwhelming need for Valium, and for a false moustache and glasses in order to get out of the building unrecognised, I had survived. Another case had been put to rest to the client's immense satisfaction … regardless of my sanity.

A couple of weeks later, at a social function, I ran into the judge who was the author of what I must admit turned out to be a good plan if you don't count my sessions with the psychiatrist. I couldn't help myself. I marched straight up to him and I said, 'You horrible man! How could you do that to me?' (I'm not particularly good at saying things which will get me ahead in my profession.)

The judge laughed, 'You should have seen your face when I told you I was releasing him into your custody!'

That judge and I have since come to an agreement. He can tell his judicial mates about the arsonist's trip to the bank whenever he likes, and I can put the story in my book. With the passage of time, that seems to be eminently reasonable. But at the time, I assure you (and I assure him through these pages) I could cheerfully have strangled him.

What Really Happened

The hardest case I have ever handled in my career involved a father accused of murdering his 17-month-old son.

The parents were a young middle-class couple, Jane and Derek, with a lovely suburban home and two beautiful children: the baby, David, and a preschool-aged girl. They had had no dealings with the law in the past.

The little boy had been unwell for a couple of weeks and had been backwards and forwards to several doctors, and to outpatients' departments, with some sort of respiratory tract infection and vomiting.

That morning, David was in Derek's care while Jane was out at work. According to Derek, little David fitted and stopped breathing. Derek said that he tried mouth-to-mouth and nose resuscitation, and then picked the infant up, flung him over his shoulder and hit him sharply between the shoulder blades (thinking that he must have swallowed something which was blocking his airway). He then called the ambulance.

I still have a copy of the 000 (911) call tape where you can hear the stertorous breathing of the dying child in the background. It is a deeply disturbing recording.

After three days in hospital, the life support was turned off and David died in his parents' arms. Shortly afterwards Derek was interviewed by police, and some months later he was charged by police with murder, the allegation being that he had lost his temper with the child and shaken him hard enough to kill him. One of the reasons it took so long to charge him was that medical reports had to be provided from several specialists following a post-mortem.

As is usual in murder charges, Derek was taken off to prison to await his trial. There was no point in applying for bail—extraordinary circumstances are required to get bail on a murder charge. The reasoning is that the potential punishment is so severe that an accused will be highly motivated to run away.

Almost all the evidence was medical—the prosecution case was based almost solely on the injuries suffered by the child, all of which were internal (brain swelling and damage, retinal bleeding and bleeding on the brain). There were no bruises, grazes, fractures or anything of that nature, either recent or older.

There was no confession and no motive.

The prosecution's argument was that the father had lost his temper with an unwell, crying baby and, despite normally being a loving parent, had shaken the child hard, causing the child's head to move violently backwards and forwards and the brain to move inside the skull causing brain damage, swelling and bleeding.

This case was going to be won or lost on the medical evidence.

The parents applied for a grant of legal aid and I agreed to take the case on, with the help of another lawyer without whose support I don't think the workload would have been possible. As it was, I spent over 600 hours in preparation for the trial.

Shaken baby syndrome

I started by learning all I could about 'shaken baby syndrome', and about the various areas of medicine covered by the prosecution statements. The more I read the more I soon realised how little I knew about the whole field—I knew I was never going to have a complete grasp of it. It became obvious to me that there was a lot of debate about just how much force it takes to create the sort of injury that young David had sustained. The prosecution version was that the sort of force required meant that the shaking had to be deliberate, but another school of thought then believed that in some circumstances these injuries could have been caused by much less force and therefore could have been caused accidentally.

We had enormous difficulty even getting any experts to review the case before the trial, as not many were interested in being seen to help a baby killer (forget the fact that he had not been convicted and was presumed innocent). Several said, 'I'm on the baby's side.' Frankly, I thought that attitude stank. I wasn't asking doctors to favour one position or another, I just wanted them to look at the materials and tell me what they thought. Surely they could be objective enough to do this. But I guess they would not be able to face their friends at the golf club.

Other specialists offered to help behind the scenes provided their colleagues did not get to hear about it. I suppose that was better than nothing.

We tried very hard to involve international researchers, as these were the people casting doubt on the more traditional theories. We offered to arrange for histopathology slides to be sent to them and to set up a satellite hookup for them to give evidence. It all came to nought. They were too busy, or unavailable for other reasons. These people were in great demand by defence lawyers around the world and it was understandable that they just wanted to get on with their work.

I don't think I have ever worked so hard in my life. I had to learn enough about the specialised medicine to ask sensible questions and understand the answers (that second bit was much harder). The only so-called experts who seemed to want to help were people with weird and wonderful theories which did not seem to have any basis other than their particular obsessions. I learnt how to spot a charlatan at 50 paces. I learnt to check that people actually had the degrees they said they had. I learnt to take nothing at face value, and that superficially plausible and impressive medical jargon often masked irrationality and emotion.

One person telephoned describing himself as a professor, and in very strong Eastern European-accented English proceeded to tell me just what crooks all the prosecution witnesses were. By the end of the conversation he had worked himself into quite a lather. I thanked him for his time and told him that I would be in touch when and if I wanted a report. Within hours, a 37-page report landed on my desk, putting the child's injuries down to a misalignment of chakras in the mother before birth, or some such nonsense. Within a few days, the expert himself had flown in from Darwin and turned up at my office without an appointment. He lambasted me for being a pathetic and hopeless lawyer because I had not got my client out on bail when he was so clearly innocent. To no avail I told the good professor that no-one, but no-one, gets out on bail on a murder charge unless the circumstances are utterly extraordinary.

He was having none of it. I lost my temper and ordered him out of my office. His parting shot was that he was going to see Jane, with whom he proposed to stay, and tell her to have me sacked. I would have been very glad to have been sacked because the amount of work involved in this trial was extraordinary and it was being done as a legal aid case, which meant that I was being paid about tuppence ha'penny per hour. However, I thought it better to ring the wife and warn her that this well-intentioned but very strange man was on his way to see her and possibly stay with her. I warned her that no professional witness would ever do this unless they wanted their credibility shot down in flames by the prosecution at trial.

Eventually, we did locate a forensic pathologist who would look at the case. He told me, in advance, that his opinion would not be helpful as the symptoms clearly indicated shaken baby syndrome. However, after reading the prosecution witness statements and the recent research I had unearthed, he changed his mind and agreed that the injuries could well have been suffered either as a direct consequence of the baby's illness, or accidentally when the father was trying to resuscitate the baby after he fitted. It looked as if we had a defence.

No sooner did we decide we could go ahead, than the pathologist became ill and had to withdraw from the case. We had to have the trial adjourned. By the time we found someone to replace him, Derek had been in prison for 20 months. During that time in custody he was labelled a baby killer and was therefore very vulnerable in the general prison population. He was attacked several times. Jane stood by him during his enforced separation from her and their three-year-old daughter.

No jury

In the weeks leading up to the trial there was a public awareness campaign running in the media about shaken baby syndrome, with television pictures of eggs whizzing round in blenders with red food colouring as an example of what happens to a baby's brain when the baby is shaken. Not very scientific, but most impressive. I was worried about how a jury might react so we asked the court for permission not to have a jury and for the client to be tried by a judge alone. Our request was granted.

The real difficulty was that the study of shaken baby syndrome or non-accidental injury was still continuing, so the medical knowledge in the reports which helped the police decide to arrest my client was in a state of flux (as it still is). By the time the trial came around there had been less certainty than there was in the beginning about what the injuries really meant. As Helen Dalley, of Channel Nine's *Sunday* program commented, 'The difficulty for both sides involved in these cases is that they have to rely on medical evidence, as there are rarely any witnesses to these events. What was sure and accepted by experts in the past may be open to question in the future.'

The prosecution had an ophthalmologist, a radiologist, an intensive care paediatrician, a forensic pathologist, a histologist, a neuropathologist, a paediatrician, a paediatric neurologist, two lawyers and an assistant. They also had professional advice and had attended a shaken baby syndrome conference.

Also on their side was the awareness campaign about the syndrome, along with the argument that 'we've all wanted to shake our kids'. In light of such an argument, Derek's good character wasn't going to help him much. The prosecution also had an unassailable sense of righteousness, and they had money.

The defence had a haematologist, a toxicologist and a forensic pathologist, me, a solicitor at the trial for some of the time, and almost no money. This was as good a position as we were ever going to be in (that is, not very good) and there was no point deferring the trial any longer. To add to my woes, the press was besieging me, I was getting very little sleep and I was trying to keep my forensic science studies going.

Several of the most important prosecution witnesses had said in their statements before the trial that they thought the medical findings indicated shaken baby syndrome, but that the ophthalmologist's report was what really tipped the scales for them and showed that the father had indisputably shaken his son to death and that it was no accident. I was really worried about this as we had not been able to find an ophthalmologist who would even look at the case, so I was going to have to try to 'shake' the ophthalmologist's evidence just by my cross-examination. I had not been able to find anyone who would even speak to me off the record about the ophthalmology evidence.

When this doctor came to the stand, I felt sick with nerves.

As he was a prosecution witness, the prosecutor asked him questions first. I had a copy of his witness statements and I was surprised that he did not seem to be saying everything that appeared in his statement. He looked a little worried and kept shuffling through what looked like printouts or photocopies.

What seems to be the problem?

I got up to cross-examine him, I still felt sick and probably was not thinking very clearly. I effectively asked him if there was something bothering him which is a pretty vague question. To my astonishment, he freely admitted that there was indeed something bothering him.

He explained that since he had given his original statement, he had done more research (hence the paper shuffling), and had found that while the infant was in intensive care the heroic efforts to save the child had produced a type of diabetes which in turn could mimic the sort of bleeding in the retina which he observed in this case. He told the court that he was no longer as sure as he had been that the child had been violently and deliberately shaken.

As he was giving this evidence the prosecutor was doing his best to keep a poker face and act as if this was all perfectly expected. I turned and looked at the investigating police officer behind me, and his face said it all. He was shocked. In fact he mouthed a four letter word

When the other crucial prosecution witness, the forensic pathologist, came to give his evidence, I asked him about the new research I had discovered before the trial and which I knew had been brought to his attention. He said, 'It may be that this concept of ... relatively non-violent shaking causing this syndrome is right but ... the jury is still out.' At this point I regretted my decision to dispense with a jury. I would have loved them to have heard those last few words.

I could not believe what I was hearing. After several more questions I finally asked him, 'is it your personal view that you would not be prepared to say that [the baby's] death was due to violent shaking?'

He answered, 'That's right.'

I sat down. I had had no ammunition, and yet it looked as if we had a real chance. In fact, although I hardly dared think it, we may have won.

The rest of the trial was just a blur to me. I really cannot remember what happened. I do know that we had to wait because when there is no jury the judge has to give written reasons for his decision. Some time later we all came back to court (the client having been transported in a prison van for the verdict) and waited for the decision. The judge said, '… it is not only possible, but likely, that the accused administered sharp blows to the back of the deceased in an attempt to dislodge whatever he thought was obstructing his son's breathing. Those blows could have caused or contributed to the cascade of events which ultimately led to the death … The evidence gave rise to considerable doubt as to whether shaking was the cause of death.'

I was astounded. As I read the judgment, I realised that not only was a judge saying that the prosecution had failed to prove Derek's guilt beyond reasonable doubt, but the judge was actually saying that he had considerable doubt. This was completely unnecessary, because as we all know, the prosecution has to prove an accused person's guilt beyond a reasonable doubt. It doesn't matter, in fact, whether the accused person is positively believed. Maybe I'm wrong, but I thought the judge might have even been saying that he was inclined to believe Derek.

After 20 months in custody, Derek was free. That was not the end. The family was not immediately reunited. There was an application by the Department of Family and Children's Services to remove the older child from the family as, despite the verdict of acquittal, they believed her to be in danger. The prosecution also appealed the judgement of acquittal. This appeal did not succeed and eventually the application to remove the older child was withdrawn.

The family was reunited, and as far as I know are still living happily together, though they have left Western Australia. I have permission from them to write about their case.

The field of shaken baby syndrome is still being actively researched and today, based on medical evidence, you will still find people who will say Derek did not deliberately and violently shake little David, and people who will say he did.

Dead Pigs and Forensics

Dead Pigs and Forensics

My first foray into the world of forensic science was on behalf of a biker, probably about 20 years ago. Representatives of a motorcycle club from New Zealand, known as the Mongrel Mob had moved to Perth, and there was concern both from police and established motorcycle enthusiasts' clubs that this overseas club might become established locally. The local bikers had been making the Mongrel Mob feel less than welcome, sometimes vigorously. The police seemed to be willing to tolerate some of this behaviour, presumably because it might persuade the New Zealanders to go home. However, some activities stretched the boundaries of what had been 'agreed' would be tolerated.

My client was seen by a security guard running from the scene of a bombing towards the car driven by his brother. The motor was running. Perhaps he mistook the guard's car for his brother's: he ran straight towards it. He stopped like a startled deer in the headlights of the guard's car, said a very rude word, and ran off again. The guard indentified him from a photo board (a cardboard folder with 12 pictures of similarly hairy ne'er-do-wells and miscreants). He was caught up with very shortly afterwards and his hands were swabbed. I was told that the Griess test carried out on the swabs revealed that explosives residue had been found on them. This seemed like a case of being caught red-handed, almost literally. I was curious about the test used, so went off to a chemistry department of a university and asked questions. The dingy walls, green linoleum covered floors, glassware and strange artificial smells reminded me of chemistry lessons in high school, some 20 years earlier. The scientists (I supposed that was who they were) all wore white lab coats and had stained shoes, presumably from dropping chemical concoctions on them.

It turned out the Griess test was a preliminary screening test. It can detect, among other things, nitroglycerine and ammonium nitrate, both of which may be found in explosives. The chemists told me that it can also give a positive result if the person has touched such common household substances as fuel additives, salami, corned beef or garden fertiliser.

We no longer had a hopeless case. In court, I asked the forensic chemist whether the results were equally consistent with having recently made a corned beef sandwich. He had to answer yes. The judge asked the prosecutor, 'You are not going to rely on that evidence, are you?'

My client was acquitted and the brother driving the getaway car was convicted.

It is a strange trick of human memory that the forensic chemist who gave prosecution evidence all those years ago recalls the events at this trial in a completely different way. He thinks the chemistry was conclusive and that my client was convicted. One day I will find the transcript and check who is actually correct.

As a matter of interest, the convictions of the Birmingham Six (a group said to have been responsible for a pub bombing in Northern Ireland) were later overturned partly on the basis that the positive reading obtained in the Griess test in that case may have come from the cellulose on the cards two of them had been playing with just before they were arrested.

My client later came back to me, having been accused of a safe cracking. No doubt this accusation was quite unfair—he was probably teaching Sunday School at the time. I thought I deserved to be rewarded for my previous efforts, so put my fees up by 10 per cent. He decided I was too expensive, went to another lawyer and was convicted. So you see, there is justice in this world. (If the truth be known, he probably would have been convicted if he had stayed with me, but why let the truth get in the way of a good story?)

Dumb and dumber

Criminals seem to be very forensically aware these days. They used to be worried about fingerprints. These days, they are all worried about DNA. Take Marvin, for example.

Fred and Marvin were two would-be bank robbers. They decided on a foolproof plan to rob a bank in a small country town. They would wait near the bank while the employees were let in before the doors were opened to the general public. Fred and Marvin were locals, so they would both wear disguises. As one of the employees was entering, they would rush in after them and rob the bank. The advantage of this cunning plan was that no members of the public would get in the way and the whole plan was much more likely to succeed than if the robbery had been carried out during normal business hours they thought.

One Monday morning, several employees had arrived very early. While carrying out their usual unlocking and sorting out duties, one of the tellers looked outside. There, sitting in the deserted shopping plaza on a low brick wall surrounding a spindly tree, were two young men dressed like the Blues Brothers: black suits, black hats, sunglasses, white shirts, narrow black ties. Just the sort of thing you would wear at 8am in a small country town outside the bank.

The teller said to one of her colleagues, 'You don't think these guys are going to rob the bank, do you?' The other answered, 'No, no-one could be that stupid.'

While Fred kept a lookout, Marvin tried to slip through the sliding doors into the bank after one of the employees. Unfortunately for Marvin, the other employees inside were waiting for him, and operated the doors to slam them shut. Marvin's hand was caught in the doors. The first job for the police when they arrived was to extract Marvin from the door, which they did, but not before he had left a large chunk of skin from one of the knuckles on his right hand in the door.

Marvin eventually found his way to me as a client. His first question, after I had read all the paperwork, including the account of what had happened, and had stopped laughing long enough to answer him, was, 'Do you think they've got my DNA?'

That set me off again: 'They don't need your DNA,' I spluttered. 'All they have to do is match the hole in your hand with a lump of skin they found on the door!'

Eventually, and very wisely, Fred and Marvin pleaded guilty. About all I could say to the judge on Marvin's behalf was that he was hardly the brains of the operation.

DNA for the defence

DNA doesn't just help the prosecution. It has its uses for the defence as well. DNA can exclude a suspect, where it can be proved the DNA at the scene absolutely does not belong to him. In the USA many people have been released from death row when biological samples (saliva, blood, semen etc) have been retested in light of advances in DNA technology. The frightening thing to think about is those who have already been executed, and those who do not have the advantage of having a biological sample available for testing. Not so long ago, I used DNA for the defence, as a threat. I have had to change what really happened just a bit in the retelling of this story, as I still see some of the people involved from time to time.

John was a schoolteacher. It was Christmas party season, and all the teachers from the school had gone to their local Irish pub to celebrate with Guinness and good cheer. It was about 11.30pm. John was not particularly drunk, but certainly would have been over the legal drink driving limit. Being a good chap, and not wanting to drink drive, he decided to walk home. (Cabs are impossible to find in the pre-Christmas period in most cities, and Perth is no exception.) It was about a 40-minute walk.

John took a shortcut through a car park belonging to a large company. This car park was patrolled by uniformed security guards. The security firms design the uniforms to look very much like police uniforms, to give an air of authority. Although the security industry is quite tightly regulated, some testosterone loaded idiots do slip through the net; people who for one reason or another are unable to gain entry into the police force, or want an easy way to exert some power. Unfortunately, John encountered one of these cowboys while taking his shortcut.

This man stepped out of the shadows and blocked John's path: 'Just where do you think you're going, matey?'

'Home.'

'The only home you're going to is a convalescent home if you don't get out of here now.' The cowboy was a comedian too.

Stupidly, John tried to reason with him. 'Look, mate, I'm just taking a shortcut—I live just over there.'

That was enough. The guard grabbed him and roughly frogmarched him towards the gate. John shouted and struggled, receiving a couple of back-handers for his trouble.

Dead Pigs and Forensics

John's next mistake was to ask, 'How do I know you're even a guard? Show me some ID.' The guard grabbed the plastic identification badge which was attached by Velcro to his blue jacket, and jammed it into my client's mouth. 'There's your fucking ID,' he snarled.

A minute or so later the police arrived. They had been called by a passerby who had seen what was happening but had not wanted to get involved. This witness disappeared before the police arrived and would not be heard from again, which is a pity, as it might have been easier to get at the truth that way. The guard immediately alleged that John had been trespassing and had attacked him.

John's night continued to get worse. He found himself at the police station, giving a statement and then being charged with assault. In fairness, in a situation where the two parties who had been present were the only ones available to give their story, the police were not totally out of line in laying charges.

The next day John found his way to my office. It's never easy to defend someone when it is one word against another. In this case it was going to be even harder, as John had had a few drinks and had been found in a place he had no right to be. However, something was nagging away at the back of my mind about the badge incident and it reminded me of something; I just couldn't think at the time what it was.

The next morning, I was in the shower, where I do some of my best thinking. Unlike one lawyer I know, however,

I don't charge my clients for under-the-shower thinking time. I mulled over the case some more. I knew John had given a statement to police where he accused the guard of acting violently towards him, including shoving the badge in his mouth, but we thought he had no one and nothing independent to back him up or corroborate him. Then it dawned on me: the badge incident reminded me of the procedure police use when they are taking a DNA sample from a suspect. They take a plastic instrument a bit like an ice cream stick, often with an absorbent section on the end, and scrape it inside a person's cheek, to get some cells from inside their mouth. This is the most convenient and least intrusive way to collect DNA.

Still dripping, I went to the phone and tracked down the arresting police officer, who (luckily) was on an early shift. When I told him my brainwave, he was very receptive to the idea. I had the impression he had not been entirely happy about charging John. We agreed that he should immediately track down the security guard, or more precisely the badge that the guard had been wearing that evening, and send it off for DNA testing.

Things moved very quickly after that. The police officer went as far as tracking down the guard and the badge, but wouldn't you know it, as soon as he told the guard what he was planning to do with the badge the guard decided he didn't want to take his allegation of assault against John any further. In fact, the guard seemed to completely lose his memory of the event. Strange, wasn't it?

Back to school

Forensic science has become an extraordinarily powerful tool in solving crimes and prosecuting criminals. Many lawyers are nervous about forensic science. Often a major reason they did law at university was because science did not come naturally to them. Like it or not, they are now being forced to deal with it in the courtroom, and some do so better than others.

I am reminded of a lawyer I watched recently cross-examining a toxicologist: 'Doctor, is it the case that the heroin in the body of the deceased had turned into some other drug?' The toxicologist, very patiently, replied, 'Are you asking me whether a metabolite of heroin, such as monoacetylmorphine or codeine was found at the injection site or anywhere in the body of the deceased?' (The significance of this, by the way, is that heroin breaks down into other substances, or metabolites, as it is processed in the body over time and therefore the toxicological findings can say something about how soon after injection the death occurred.) This lawyer, defender of the innocent, scourge of the wrongful prosecution, general all-round hero, answered, 'I don't know, am I?' And he took good money for this! To this day, he probably doesn't know how badly he is letting his clients down.

Another lawyer, when confronted with a case which depended mainly upon medical evidence, told his client, 'You can't argue with doctors. We are going to have to defend you based on your previous good character.' That is not much to defend a murder charge on.

Of course lawyers can argue with doctors. Lawyers can argue with anyone. That's what they are trained to do and paid a fee to do. The fact that it's science they are arguing about doesn't—or shouldn't—make any difference. I realise it's easy for me to say this as I have a science background, but like it or not, lawyers and judges are having to confront science. Some take it head-on. Others are being dragged kicking and screaming into it.

I was always fascinated by forensic science, but as time went on I realised that the knowledge I had picked up from various trials just wasn't enough. The more trials involving forensic evidence I did, the more I realised just how little I knew. I was worried about what I had missed in the past and what I might miss in the future if I didn't get my skills up to date.

Probably because I had been fretting about this I noticed an advertisement in the newspaper offering a Masters Degree in Forensic Science. There were no such degrees for lawyers. It was designed for science graduates, so at least technically, I was eligible. My first degree was, indeed, in science although I had graduated about 25 years earlier and the science was psychology, not physics or chemistry. Mere details.

I enrolled. I kept on working full-time and did the course full-time as well. It was an enormously hard workload, but great fun. Every subject taught me something extraordinary and I am very glad that I took on the challenge.

Forensic chemistry was especially scary. I had last studied chemistry at high school over 30 years earlier. On day one, I walked into the building, which smelt of strange scientific stuff, and into the lecture theatre. I looked around and was relieved to find a chart on the wall, known as the Periodic Table of elements, familiar to high school students the world over. 'Great,' I thought, 'I know what this thing is.' Then I looked at it more closely. I couldn't believe it: there were at least half a dozen more elements than existed in my day. They had shifted the goalposts! I sat through the entire chemistry course in a daze, and only passed because I knew how to write a decent essay. I really had no idea what was going on. But it was still fun.

Warped humour and 'frenzied entomology'

I have mentioned elsewhere that criminal lawyers and police develop a fairly warped sense of humour, partly as a result of the type of work they do. Their sense of humour is positively mainstream compared to that of forensic pathologists, though. An end-of-semester barbecue was being held at the university for the forensic science students. Some of the lecturers were there, including one of the pathologists. A student had brought his wife and new baby in, and asked whether the pathologist would like to hold the baby. His answer? 'No, I'm only good with dead babies.' What really worries me about this remark, however, is that I am not sure it was meant to be a joke.

I have a deal with a good friend of mine who is also a forensic pathologist. She has promised me that if I have to be 'cut up' at her place of work, they will leave my clothes on for as long as possible and deal with me in a private room. It might be the only time I get a private room in hospital, so I appreciate her offer.

I have had some orthodontic treatment over the last few years, and as a result need to wear a plastic retainer, a bit like a mouth guard, moulded to fit the shape of my teeth. I can't eat with it in, and it is very easy to lose, as it is clear plastic. Being female, I often have no pockets in my clothing, so when I take it out, I shove it in my bra, so as not to lose it. Then I usually forget it's there until I get changed for bed. I have told my friend that if I am found with an apparent bite mark on my left breast, it may not be what it seems, and she should check it against my own teeth.

The subject of forensic entomology became known among my fellow students as 'frenzied entomology'. We had to make an insect collection which involved running around with a butterfly net, or buying collections from students of previous years, or paying young children 20 cents per bug. I learnt the shortcuts too late, so I did it the hard way. Having caught the insects, we then had to kill them. The way to do this was to use a screw-top jar with pieces of cotton wool soaked in acetone (nail polish remover) in the bottom. You put the insect in the jar and it dies humanely (or insectly). If you don't have time to kill it immediately, you shove it in a jar in the fridge and the low temperature induces it to wait quietly and patiently for its big moment.

Once killed, the next trick is to use itsy bitsy little pins and pin the corpse into some foam for display. The real trick is to do it without the insect falling apart. You have to figure out exactly what sort of insect it is and bung its scientific name on the label in itsy bitsy writing. This label goes on the pin too. If you manage to catch some big meaty insect like a Bogong, you have to disembowel it and stuff it with cotton wool, and still manage to keep it intact. Now that is my idea of fun.

Possibly my worst insect-collecting experience was the day I collected, refrigerated, "killed" and then pinned a moth. It wasn't that meaty, so I did not bother gutting it. An hour or so after I had pinned it, I heard scrabbling from inside the cardboard box where the collection lived. I opened the box, and there, impaled on a pin, was my moth, desperately flapping to get free. It seemed I had not used enough acetone and had not "killed" the moth. It hadn't noticed it was being pinned, presumably because it was refrigerated. I poured a big splash from a jar of acetone directly over the top of the moth. The acetone then ate away half the foam. I should have just bought my insect collection, as some of the other students had done.

One major triumph involved dissecting cockroaches. It seems that there are girl cockroaches and boy cockroaches.

It is not particularly easy to tell the difference, unless you are a cockroach hero like me! Not only did I learn to tell the difference between girl and boy cockroaches from the outside, but I also learnt to dissect them and tell the difference from the inside. I had no idea that boy cockroaches have weird little fluffy cotton wool-like testes inside them. I realised I was really getting sucked in to the world of entomology when I actually got excited about finding these little gems. I have absolutely no idea what the point of the exercise was, and I don't think I will ever again need to use this knowledge (cockroaches are a bit like constitutional law in that respect), but it was, in a perverse sort of way, really good fun. It probably stems from my days as a toddler when I used to sit at the bottom of the venetian blinds in my grandmother's house and thread bodies of dead blowflies onto knitting needles.

Dr Piglove

The person who taught 'frenzied entomology' bore the nickname Dr Piglove. There was a fairly gross reason for this, which soon became all too clear. One of the areas forensic entomologists work in is PMI (Post Mortem Interval or 'How long has this person been dead?'). Obviously in criminal investigations the date of death is often crucial. The first lecture was entitled 'Have you ever Dated a Dead Person?' I was fascinated from the very start. How could I not be, with a title like that?

Entomologists estimate the post-mortem interval by looking at the insect infestation on the body. They look at what maggots are on the body, how big and developed they are (that is, how old they are), whether there are other insects, and anything else revolting they can think of. Maggots are the larvae of flies. Once someone is dead, flies tend to arrive pretty quickly. The timing of their arrival depends on any number of things, such as whether there are any open wounds, whether the person is clothed or not and whether the person is in the open or not. There is a place in the USA, in the state of Tennessee, which is popularly known as 'the Body Farm'. There, people who have left their remains to science are used to add to the body of knowledge about PMI. They are left in the open, clothed or unclothed, buried or not, in the shade, in the sun and any variation you can think of. The insect life and the rate of decomposition, among other things, are studied.

We don't do this sort of work with human bodies in Australia. The general public would just get too upset. But we do use 45-kilogram pigs, the closest thing we have to humans. Of course, people don't necessarily die naked, so some of these pigs have to be clothed. If you have the strange sense of humour a forensic scientist requires, there is nothing funnier than the sight of a dead pig wearing a pair of board shorts and a Bart Simpson T-shirt, unless it is a dead pig wearing a skirt and a brassiere. By the way, the old trick sometimes described in crime books—using Vicks VapoRub under your nose to deal with the smell—works like a charm.

Dr Piglove acquired his name by assisting one of his colleagues in a manner far beyond the call of duty. Forensic odontologists look at bite marks on humans, dead or alive. There are not many dead humans available to bite, and not many live humans happy about being bitten, even in the name of science. Hence the good old pig is called into action again. There is still a problem: how many people are willing to bite dead pigs? There is only one I know of: Dr Piglove. I have the photograph to prove it.

The best way to sum up the course was a year spent learning strange stuff, taught by strange people.

I did quite well in the course, however, and as a result was invited to enrol in a PhD.

A new career

'Yes,' I said, not really thinking about the consequences, 'I'll do a PhD.' The next problem was what on earth could I research that would fit under the 'forensic science' heading, considering that my only undergraduate science was an extremely ancient psychology degree. The only thing I could think of was looking at how juries handle scientific evidence. With the proliferation of forensic evidence in courts, and the number of CSI-type programs on television, I thought this could be fascinating.

In Australia, as in England and Canada, people are not allowed to ask jurors about their deliberations without special permission from the Attorney General. Jurors don't give interviews on the courtroom steps like we see in the USA, nor do they write books about what really happened in the jury room. I was lucky (and trusted) enough to get that permission, and have been able to speak to many jurors about their experiences. I am bilingual: I speak both law and science. This puts me in good position to make sense of what I am hearing. It is fascinating work and I expect to change the justice system by next week at the latest. Changing the world will take another week or two.

The next project is now finished as well, and it is even more fascinating. I am looking at the question of whether jurors are intimidated into giving certain verdicts. This has come about because there have been several trials over the last few years involving well-known people suspected of being involved in organised crime of one form or another, and they have been acquitted. The comment has been made that the jury must have been intimidated into their verdict. I am surveying over 3000 jurors to find out whether intimidation happens, how often it happens, what form it takes and where it comes from.

These projects and the forensic science studies I have done have led me into university teaching. As a barrister I still do the occasional forensically interesting trial.

Many lawyers have never learnt how to present forensic

evidence. They need to know how to locate someone reputable and expert in the particular field of science, because they usually have no scientific training, despite the huge rise in the use of such evidence. People are potentially being convicted or acquitted wrongly because lawyers don't know enough about science: it's scary.

When I talked to jurors during my research about expert evidence, the dangers of the knowledge deficit among lawyers became more apparent. I found that jurors wanted to ask questions about scientific and medical evidence in court because lawyers hadn't asked the right questions.

Lawyers need knowledge about forensic science. They need to understand when a case requires forensic evidence. They need to understand the reports that scientists give them. They need to know what questions to ask and be able to understand the answers. They need to know when the wool is being pulled over their eyes. And they need to be able to package all that in a way that's easily understood by the jury, because the jurors are the people who make the decisions.

I am now back at Western Australia's Murdoch University, as an associate professor in forensic science. I teach scientists how to communicate with juries, and am running a postgraduate course for lawyers teaching them the fundamentals of forensic science. The university was farsighted enough to find the funding and create a position for three years for me just so I could put this project into action. We are into our second year of the first of these postgraduate courses, the first of their kind in Australia as far as I know. We have over 20 (and counting) highly motivated and interested students of varying levels of experience and varying backgrounds: prosecutors, defence lawyers, police, an occupational health and safety expert and a forensic pathologist. What an asset they will be to the justice system in the future!

I am earning much less money than when I was in full-time legal practice, but I am having great fun (when I am not working all night), and I believe I am making a contribution that will improve the delivery of justice in Western Australia. When some people are starting to think about retirement, I'm starting a new career!

From Rats to Chateaux

One of the benefits of working in forensic science is that I travel overseas from time to time, as so much of the leading research is done outside Australia. It is a privilege to bring this knowledge back and to feel part of a global forensic community. Because I'm normally travelling on a university budget, I try to conserve money wherever I can.

Sometimes I take this attitude a little too far. London, for example, is an extremely expensive place to stay. To economise, I look at the internet hotel booking sites and grab a bargain wherever I can. I recall finding a hotel in Kensington, which is a very pleasant part of London, for 50 pounds per night. You know what they say: if something seems to be too good to be true, it probably is.

This little hotel was squeezed between a pizza parlour and a pub. The front door, three concrete steps up from footpath level, was about the size of the normal household bedroom door, but made of amber-coloured glass with wire reinforcing embedded in it. The reinforcing had not prevented a spider web of cracks radiating out from a hole in the lower part of the door. It looked as though someone had kicked the door extremely hard with a pair of steel-capped boots. I pushed hard on the aluminium handle.

The door scraped open across the puckered, filthy carpet. Luckily I only had one suitcase, which I dragged up the concrete steps and manoeuvred around the door. The long, dimly lit corridor led to a wooden cubicle. The cubicle sported a window with a perforated central disc, much like the reinforced or bulletproof glass screens you see in front of tellers at banks. This seemed to be the reception desk. A grimy white plastic doorbell was attached by Velcro to the customer side of the cubicle. There was no-one to be seen, so I pressed it. A hugely obese, middle-aged Indian chap appeared and perched on the torn vinyl stool on the other side. 'Yeeeeth?' he lisped.

I passed my booking confirmation form through the slot at the base of the window, and in exchange the key attached by string to a cardboard tag was handed over. 'Room 54, no noise after 10,' Mr Talkative said, gesturing to some stairs to one side of his 'office'. I contemplated calling for the bellboy or asking for assistance, but then reality struck. There was no way there was such an animal as a bellboy and no way my host was going to help.

I dragged my suitcase to the stairs and started climbing. And climbing. Room 54 was on the fifth floor. There was no lift. The timber stairs creaked as I climbed. There seemed to be four rooms off each landing. It was a hot evening and I was extremely hot by the time I reached my room. I stopped and checked the room number: yes, there was a little chrome '54' screwed to the grotty beige door. The base of the door was stained and splintered as if there had been a flood, though I could not work out how this could have occurred on the fifth floor. The muggy, musty smell which I first noticed at 'reception' intensified. The door opened easily and I walked into my 'Deluxe ensuite single accommodation'. In this room were:

1 x single bed with a plastic mattress protector

1 x rubber pillow

2 x sheets so worn they were almost transparent

1 x coarse grey army-style blanket

1 x sliver of soap

1 x brittle plastic disposable tumbler.

That was all.

The so-called ensuite was a shower in a sort of cupboard, with no curtain, over a small drain hole in the floor. There was no risk it would flood as it bore a rough cardboard sign dangling from a string, upon which was scribbled in pencil: 'OUT OF OREDER. USE FACILITES IN HOTTEL NEX DOOR.' Forget it. I was hot and sweaty but I would live.

The heat rose up the stairwell, but the miniature window could not be opened. I was jetlagged, and had just struggled up five flights of stairs with my suitcase, so I simply lay on the bed with as few clothes as I could manage, and tried to sleep.

As I started to doze, I was roused by a rhythmic thumping from the next room. I could make out two voices, one male and one female. After a time the thumping stopped. The door outside banged, the voices started again, and the stairs creaked as people climbed up and down them. The creaking stairs, the rhythmic thumping and the banging doors continued for the rest of the evening and most of the night. It slowly dawned on me that it was not only the doors that were banging. The other occupants clearly rented their rooms by the hour, not the evening.

From brothels to men's clubs

The next time I went to London I thought I would try a safer way of economising. I belonged to a club which had a reciprocal accommodation deal with some London clubs, which meant that you could stay in the centre of London for quite a modest price. The most convenient and reasonably priced club was the Royal East India Public Schools Club. With a name like that, I had in mind pith helmets and beatings (not that I was looking for either of these fringe benefits, mind you).

This place had quite a grand entrance off a very civilised square. Upon entering the slightly faded lobby, I spotted a noticeboard which spelled out the rules of conduct. It seemed I had to wear a jacket and tie to breakfast and that none of my lady friends were permitted upstairs in my room. One section of the noticeboard had little welcome messages to the house guests. Mine was addressed to Mr Fordham. Only men were permitted to be members of this club.

To their credit, once I had explained that I was a girl not a boy, they were quite happy still to have me. I was given the key to my room and entered the creaking lift up to the first floor, where my room was located. Each side of the wide passageway leading to the room was lined with glass display cases containing stuffed rhinos, elephants' feet, and indeed any animal that a pukka sahib might have shot in India many years ago. It was extremely disconcerting walking between the glassy-eyed beasts, especially at night. Seriously spooky.

I thought that before I wandered out for the evening I should freshen up, so decided to have a shower. This shower was located over the bath. The fact that there was a shower at all was a bonus, as baths are far more common in older establishments. After a few minutes under the shower I was disturbed by a loud banging on my door. Dripping wet, with a towel around me I answered it. It was the manager. Would I kindly, immediately, turn off the shower, as it was flooding his office, which was just below my room. It seems there was no sealant between the shower and the floor as no-one was seriously expected to use the shower. Mr Fordham did not make herself very popular, but I have to say that considering the amount of damage I apparently caused to the office below, in the great British stiff upper lip tradition, the staff were very decent to me. It was many steps up from the brothel experience!

Fordham the terrorist

Aside from weird hotels and lodging houses, London has something very special to recommend it: it is the second-hand dress and shoe shop capital of the world. The astute reader may have noticed that I have a bit of a weakness for retail therapy in general and shoes in particular. However, you can take the girl out of poverty, but not poverty out of the girl. I am an expert at second-hand clothes shopping, and these skills having been finely honed during the times spent scouring St Vinnies in the bad old days. In London, the trick is to head for the shops clustered in the small side streets around Harrods. There the glitterati dispose of their once-worn Chanels, Diors, Tods, Pradas, Guccis, and most importantly, Manolo Blahniks and Jimmy Choos. [Note to males reading this section: ask a woman, any woman and she will tell you the significance of the preceding sentence].

I would like to see some proper scientific research done about the release of endorphins ('feel good' hormones) during shopping. I would be very happy to offer myself as a subject for this research. I'm sure shoes are much safer than any other drug.

The fun of shopping overseas takes the sting out of travel dramas, like security at airports, which has become much tighter in recent years. A couple of years ago I was on a domestic flight in the USA. I was buckled into my seat ready for take-off, my tray table was up and my seat was in the upright position. Suddenly, two burly men in uniform with guns strapped to their hips entered the plane: 'Is there a Judith Fordham on the plane?' Well, I guess there was, so I raised my hand. It was pretty obvious they were security or police or sky marshals or some such thing, so when they asked me to accompany them, I did.

I was quite scared and hugely embarrassed walking past all the other passengers. I had heard of people being thrown into US prisons for being cheeky to immigration or airline officials and having to be extracted by the Australian Embassy a week or two later. Joking about bombs, for example, was likely to get you sent to Guantanamo Bay. But I had been polite to everyone!

I was taken by these two gentlemen to a pile of luggage on a trolley directly under the plane, yet to be loaded. Passengers' faces were pressed to the window, watching.

'Is that your bag, ma'am?' one of them asked, polite even to someone they were about to arrest.

'Yes, it is. Why?'

'It seems to be buzzing.'

Sure enough, a buzzing noise was coming from the top of the suitcase, and when I placed my hand on it I could feel a vibration. I was puzzled, but opened the suitcase. As I unzipped it, the buzzing noise became louder. Then, the source became clear. I had packed my suitcase the night before, leaving out some basics, including my toothbrush. Once I had cleaned my teeth I popped my toothbrush into the top of the bag at the last minute. It was an electric toothbrush, and the baggage handling had somehow turned it on.

Every time I tell people this tale, I have to insist—it was DEFINITELY a toothbrush, NOTHING else. Really. Just because it was vibrating ... why is everyone laughing?

In retrospect, I think it was pretty silly of these two men to have me open my suitcase directly under the plane. If it had been a bomb, that was not a smart move. I did wonder where they had carried out their anti-terrorist training. Perhaps through a correspondence school or an internet $5 degree site.

Travelled a long way

I haven't ever got over the feeling, instilled in me throughout my childhood, that one day people are going to realise that I am not as competent as I seem but that I'm just really good at faking it. I'm told that is called 'imposter syndrome' and that it is suffered by many women. Having said that, if I am so good at faking it, that proves I'm really competent at something …

There are plenty of downsides to that feeling, but one upside is that it keeps me grounded. I never take things for granted, am grateful for everything, and seize every opportunity which comes my way.

I don't suffer fools gladly, and with me, what you see is what you get. I am not a social butterfly, but have a circle of close and loyal friends who know exactly who they are dealing with. I think I sometimes offend people by saying exactly what I think. I don't do it to be obnoxious: it simply doesn't occur to me to do anything else, until I realise I have once again put my foot in it. That quality was forged during the times I had to choose between being crushed by circumstance or surviving. And surviving, especially when you have children, is not a question of bravery or even of choice. There is no other option.

From Rats to Chateaux

Aside from business travel John and I travel for pleasure, going overseas about once every 18 months. We go to France quite often. I said to him on one occasion, 'I'm sick of the chateau we normally stay at: let's stay at a different one this time.' Then I had a sort of out-of-body experience and heard what I was saying. I thought, 'Who the hell does she think she is? What a princess!' Then I thought again, 'I've paid my dues. If I want to bitch about staying in the same boring old chateau, I will.'

I get a bit short-tempered sometimes when people who have never experienced it say, 'Adversity is character building.' I usually retort, 'I have enough character, thank you very much, and I wouldn't mind having it easy for a while!' The way I see it, if I can deal with rats nibbling at my toes, I can enjoy chateaux. And champagne. And shoes. Don't forget shoes.

About the author

Judith Fordham commenced her career in science. She is a workaholic who later studied law as a single parent, then founded and ran her own law firm for far too long. She became a barrister then discovered the error of her ways, and is now an associate professor at the University of Western Australia teaching Forensic Science and Criminal Investigations.

Judith regularly lectures in evidence to detectives at the WA Police Academy and in expert evidence to police forensic training courses. She gives guest lectures for anyone who will buy her lunch, including the Australian College of Legal Medicine, WA and Queensland Police fingerprint, blood stain patterns and other analysts and WA and Queensland forensic scientists. She has also lectured and spoken internationally in the UK and US on the CSI Effect, Shaken Baby Syndrome and her jury research.

Judith is in the final stages of a research project on jurors, juries and expert evidence, and has completed a study on juror intimidation at the State Attorney General's personal request. She has gained permission for almost unprecedented access to jurors for post-trial interviews, normally illegal in Australia.

She continues to practise as a senior barrister handling cases with major forensic content. In her spare time she teaches advocacy and is a past President of the Australian & New Zealand Association for Psychiatry, Psychology

& Law (WA), a past President of the Criminal Lawyers Association of WA, President of the Australian and New Zealand Forensic Science Society (WA) and member of the Council of the WA Law Society, among many other groups. She is also a Member of the American Academy of Forensic Sciences.

Judith has been a guest speaker for groups such as the Princess Margaret Hospital Women of the West, South Coast Regional Chambers of Commerce Women of Vision, Leaders of Tomorrow (1200 children!), the Cancer Council, Women in Policing and Wesfarmers Senior Executive Forum. She was honoured to be made a life member of angelhands, a group formed to assist secondary victims of homicide, in recognition of her work in its establishment.

Her publications include *Doctors Orders or Patient Choice* (a book about patients' rights in medical treatment), chapters in several legal advice publications such as *Your Body, Your Baby* and *The Law Handbook WA*, academic journal articles as well as a chapter on jurors, juries and expert evidence in *Law & Psychology* (OUP 2006).

Also from New Holland ...

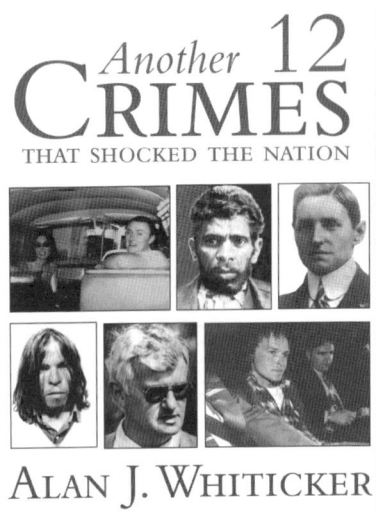

ISBN 9781741104943

ISBN 9781741102338

ISBN 9781741105278

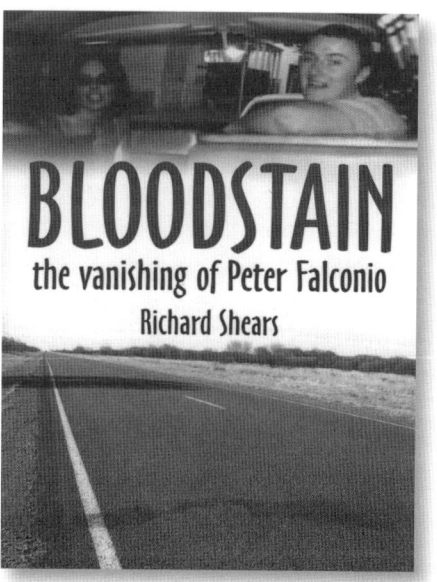

ISBN 9781741103229